The Carols of Christmas
Volume 3

Daily Advent Devotions on
Classic Christmas Carols

Alan Vermilye

The Carols of Christmas Volume 3
Daily Advent Devotions on Classic Christmas Carols

Copyright © 2024 Alan Vermilye
Brown Chair Books

ISBN-13 Paperback: 978-1-948481-44-1
ISBN-13 Hardback: 978-1-948481-46-5

To learn more about this book or to order additional copies, visit www.BrownChairBooks.com.

Scriptures taken from the Holy Bible, New International Version®, NIV®. Copyright © 1973, 1978, 1984, 2011 by Biblica, Inc.TM Used by permission of Zondervan. All rights reserved worldwide. www.zondervan.com The "NIV" and "New International Version" are trademarks registered in the United States Patent and Trademark Office by Biblica, Inc.TM

Scripture quotations marked (TLB) are taken from *The Living Bible*, copyright © 1971 by Tyndale House Foundation. Used by permission of Tyndale House Publishers, Carol Stream, Illinois 60188. All rights reserved.

Scripture taken from the New King James Version®. Copyright © 1982 by Thomas Nelson. Used by permission. All rights reserved.

Scripture quotations marked CSB have been taken from the Christian Standard Bible®, Copyright © 2017 by Holman Bible Publishers. Used by permission. Christian Standard Bible® and CSB® are federally registered trademarks of Holman Bible Publishers.

Scripture quotations are from The ESV® Bible (The Holy Bible, English Standard Version®), copyright © 2001 by Crossway, a publishing ministry of Good News Publishers. Used by permission. All rights reserved.

Scripture is taken from GOD'S WORD®.
© 1995, 2003, 2013, 2014, 2019, 2020 by God's Word to the Nations Mission Society. Used by permission.

No part of this work may be reproduced or transmitted in any form or by any means, electronic or mechanical, including photocopying and recording, or by any information storage or retrieval system, except as may be expressly permitted by the 1976 Copyright Act in writing from the publisher.

All rights reserved.
Version 1

Contents

	Introduction	VI
1.	Week 1, Day 1 Come, Thou Long Expected Jesus—A History	1
3.	Week 1, Day 2 Come, Thou Long Expected Jesus	10
4.	Week 1, Day 3 Born To Set Thy People Free	12
5.	Week 1, Day 4 From Our Fears And Sins Release Us	15
6.	Week 1, Day 5 Hope Of All The Earth Thou Art	18
7.	Week 1, Day 6 Dear Desire Of Every Nation	21
8.	Week 1, Day 7 Joy Of Every Longing Heart	24
9.	Week 2, Day 8 It Came Upon the Midnight Clear—A History	26
11.	Week 2, Day 9 It Came Upon The Midnight Clear, That Glorious Song of Old	34

12. Week 2, Day 10   36
    Peace On Earth, Good Will To Men, From Heaven's All-Gracious King

13. Week 2, Day 11   39
    Still Through The Cloven Skies They Come With Peaceful Wings Unfurled

14. Week 2, Day 12   42
    O Rest Beside The Weary Road And Hear The Angels Sing!

15. Week 2, Day 13   44
    Yet With The Woes Of Sin And Strife The World Has Suffered Long

16. Week 2, Day 14   47
    Oh, Hush the Noise, Ye Men of Strife and Hear the Angels Sing

17. Week 3, Day 15   49
    What Child Is This?—A History

20. Week 3, Day 16   56
    What Child Is This, Who, Laid to Rest

21. Week 3, Day 17   59
    This, This Is Christ The King

22. Week 3, Day 18   62
    Why Lies He In Such Mean Estate

23. Week 3, Day 19   65
    The Silent Word Is Pleading

24. Week 3, Day 20   68
    So Bring Him Incense, Gold, And Myrrh

25. Week 3, Day 21   71
    The King of Kings, Salvation Brings

26.	Week 4, Day 22 Angels From The Realms Of Glory—A History	73
29.	Week 4, Day 23 Angels From The Realms Of Glory	82
30.	Week 4, Day 24 Shepherds, In The Field Abiding	85
31.	Week 4, Day 25 Sages, Leave Your Contemplations	88
32.	Week 4, Day 26 Saints, Before The Altar Bending	91
33.	Week 4, Day 27 Sinners, Wrung With True Repentance	94
34.	Week 4, Day 28 Come And Worship, Come And Worship	96

Introduction

It brings me great joy to offer you the third and final volume of *The Carols of Christmas* devotional series. Driven by the overwhelming success of volumes 1 and 2, I set out to discover four additional carols with intriguing backstories and enough biblical content to craft a week of devotions. Fortunately, my search ended in success!

I have thoroughly enjoyed the research and writing process for all three volumes. My appreciation for each carol deepened as I uncovered the captivating narratives and historical influences that shaped each melody and their lasting impact on culture. This journey has been nothing short of amazing, and I feel immensely grateful that God has given me the opportunity to share it with you.

Similar to my approach in the previous volumes, I dedicated myself to conducting thorough research, understanding that discrepancies might arise in the narratives of hymns that have spanned more than a hundred years. Then I divided them into four weeks of daily devotions for Christmas. You will start each week by reading the history of the carol, followed by six daily devotions. Although Advent usually starts on the fourth Sunday before Christmas, the devotions in this book are undated and can be started anytime.

To enhance your reading, I've also prepared free resources such as a small group discussion guide, a podcast offering extra carol history, and weekly devotionals on the carols. To access these free resources, go to BrownChairBooks.com/free.

Since releasing the first volume of *The Carols of Christmas*, I've had the pleasure of receiving countless stories from readers who have enjoyed these devotional books. It would be a joy to hear your story as well. Please drop me a note on the contact page at www.brownchairbooks.com. In addition, I would be extremely grateful if you could take a moment to review the book on Amazon. Your review would greatly benefit both me and other readers who are curious to know if this devotional is a good fit for them.

God Bless and Merry Christmas!

Alan

Week 1, Day 1

COME, THOU LONG EXPECTED JESUS—A HISTORY

The setting was London, England, in the eighteenth century, shortly before the advent of the Industrial Revolution. Half of the population was living in dire conditions, with the poorest families squeezed into single-room dwellings. Despite advancements in farming, most people couldn't afford to purchase meat and survived mainly on bread, butter, potatoes, and tea. The absence of government assistance led to challenges for many in obtaining basic necessities such as food and shelter.

To make matters worse, the statistics revealed a somber reality: Nearly half of the children born during this period, roughly five hundred out of every one thousand, didn't survive past their second birthday. Malnutrition, unclean water, contaminated food, and inadequate hygiene practices were the leading causes of this heart-wrenching outcome. Those children that managed to survive were frequently left homeless and abandoned on the streets, their lack of education making it difficult for them to improve their circumstances. The increase in homeless children led to the creation of institutions known as orphanages, which primarily operated as workhouses.

Workhouses were grim places with cruel house masters that frequently forced children to do tasks that no one else would even think of doing. Children endured unimaginable mistreatment at the hands of their masters—beaten, starved, and subjected to various forms of abuse.

Typically, children remained in workhouses until around the age of twelve, at which point they would either become an apprentice or join the military. Some, who couldn't tolerate the work anymore, would flee into the streets and join gangs, commonly known as Blackguard Children. Unfortunately, the girls had a slightly worse fate, with most of them turning to prostitution if they weren't adopted.

This was the unfortunate reality of life in eighteenth century England and one that Charles Wesley was all too familiar with. He and his brother John had been tirelessly preaching the gospel across the country and had witnessed firsthand the exploitation of children and the horrible conditions they endured. While sitting on a train coach in 1744, he couldn't help but ponder the profound sense of injustice that surrounded him. In his discouragement, he clung to Haggai's reminder to the Israelites that God's power can transform a bleak present into a future filled with unimaginable glory.[1]

While traveling on the train that day, Wesley found himself deeply moved and motivated to write a prayer that would capture the profound needs and longings of humanity as well as the hopeful anticipation of Christ's imminent return to restore justice and bring about complete renewal. It was a prayer filled with eager anticipation, reminding believers of Christ's first coming to Bethlehem and their longing for his future return. The inspiration he found would live on as a cherished Christmas carol, touching the hearts of millions for over 275 years.

---

1. Haggai 2:9

Charles Wesley was an English Methodist leader and considered one of the greatest hymn writers of all time, having penned in his lifetime over 6,000 hymns and some 3,000 poems. He was the brother of John Wesley, the famous theologian and founder of Methodism, who once said that his brother's hymnal was the best theological book in existence. We still sing some of Wesley's famous hymns today, including "Christ the Lord Is Risen Today," "Hark! The Herald Angels Sing," and "O for a Thousand Tongues to Sing."

Shortly after writing his prayer, Wesley adapted it into a rather short, two-stanza hymn and published it in his *Hymns for the Nativity of Our Lord* hymnal that same year. While the hymn was initially not well known outside of Methodist circles, it gained broader recognition when it was included in a collection of hymns known as festival hymns. These hymns reached beyond the Methodist community and were sung at communal gatherings to bring people together for worship, where they would sing, read, and pray. Interestingly, it took more than a century for the hymn to become widely popular across various Christian denominations. This was due primarily to a famous Baptist preacher who featured it as an illustration in his Christmas sermon in London.

Charles Spurgeon, famously known as the "Prince of Preachers," preached to over ten million people during his lifetime, making him the most popular preacher of his day. He authored numerous theology books and wrote over 3,500 sermons that are now bound in sixty-three volumes. At the young age of twenty-one, in 1855, a mere five years after his conversion, he had already taken charge of the largest Baptist church in London and was quickly becoming a well-known figure. In that year's Christmas sermon, Spurgeon used Wesley's hymn to illustrate his point that very few are born a king, Jesus, of course, being the sole exception in that he had been born a king without ever being a prince.

Following that, the hymn quickly gained popularity and was incorporated into the hymnals of both the Church of England and American churches. However, it wasn't until 1875 that it was finally included in the Methodist Wesleyan Hymn Book, after previously being excluded. The original reason for exclusion stemmed from the fact that no officially suitable music had been created for it prior to that. Wesley's original choice of melody for the hymn remains a mystery, and it has been performed with various melodies over time. Many consider "Stuttgart," a beautiful composition by German composer Christian Friedrich Witt, to be the very first tune ever used, but it wasn't until the mid-1800s that the popular lyrics became paired in most hymnals with a stirring Welsh melody, albeit one meant for children.

In 1844 Rowland Hugh Prichard, a nineteen-year-old Welsh musician, composed the melody "Hyfrydol" for his children's songbook titled *The Singer's Friend*, which also included forty other tunes. Despite spending most of his life working in the textile industry, Prichard was widely recognized for his exceptional singing ability and his role as a choir director. He was also a lesser-known individual who contributed to the advancement of Welsh hymn singing in the mid-1800s.

Hyfrydol, a term that means cheerfulness, beauty, and melody, presented a striking contrast to the traditionally stately "Stuttgart" melody. The melody became immensely popular and has been featured in over four hundred hymnals, with various adaptations. It can be heard in hymns such as "Alleluia! Sing to Jesus" by William Chatterton Dix, Charles Wesley's "Love Divine, All Loves Excelling," and Francis Harold Rowley's "I Will Sing the Wondrous Story," among numerous other hymns from diverse church traditions. While some traditions still sing Wesley's carol with the "Stuttgart" melody, the "Hyfrydol" melody is the most widely recognized version heard today.

Today "Come, Thou Long-Expected Jesus" is considered a lesser-known carol that is rarely played on the radio, heard in shopping malls, or unfortunately sung as frequently in church services as other carols. Actually, it's quite possible that you won't hear its rousing call for Jesus to come at all during the Christmas season. And in the event that you do hear the carol, it's unlikely that you'll be as familiar with the lyrics as you would be with "Silent Night," "Joy to the World," or other more popular carols.

It could be that we've grown so accustomed to our Christmas carols incorporating certain elements of the nativity that are never actually mentioned in Wesley's hymn. Although the word "born" is used four times, there's no reference to Mary, Joseph, Bethlehem, shepherds, wise men, or mangers. Though there are angels.

Ironically, though, among all the Christmas carols, there couldn't be one more fitting for the Advent season than one that begins with the inviting word "Come." Advent traces its roots back to the Latin term "adventus," which directly translates to "coming" or "arrival." Christmas is not only about celebrating the coming of Jesus at his birth but also our hope and anticipation of his second coming.

The words we sing in "Come, Thou Long-Expected Jesus" have remained virtually unchanged since Wesley first published it in the 1700s. This is a significant departure from other carols, as many have undergone subtle or dramatic changes and additions over the years. As you read through the lyrics, you begin to understand the reasons behind it. The theological richness and significance of Wesley's prayer, written over two centuries ago, remains just as captivating, poetic, and applicable in the present day.

Despite the challenging circumstances in which it was written, Charles Wesley's beautiful hymn resonates through time, offering peace and inspiration. Like Wesley, we, too, can examine the decline of culture in modern times, the attack on Christian values and principles, international conflicts, and the persisting challenges in our own lives that leave us feeling overwhelmed and in need of deliverance, peace, and hope.

As Wesley sat on the train that day, he shared the same sentiment. While he and his brother John were actively involved in various social causes, such as ending slavery, improving prison conditions, assisting the underprivileged, and promoting education for all, he couldn't overlook the vast amount of injustice that still needed to be rectified in his own town. In the midst of feeling overwhelmed, he turned to the comforting words of Scripture and sought solace through prayer. And being the prolific writer that he was, he then meticulously transcribed his prayer, ensuring that others could recite the same words and intentions.

Wesley's prayer, both simple and profound, has resonated with millions of people for over 275 years, being spoken, prayed, and sung. As the music plays, some sing with pure delight, enchanted by the beautiful lyrics and harmonious melody, while others, weary from enduring seasons of waiting, are desperately pleading for the Lord to come into their own broken lives, bringing strength, joy, and peace.

Regardless of your familiarity with the carol, its lyrics and melody will undoubtedly touch you. As you enter this Advent season, where do you find yourself? Is there an injustice that breaks your heart and compels you to call upon Jesus to come? Drawing inspiration from Wesley, it might be beneficial to start by recalling the teachings of Scripture. Then seek spiritual guidance through prayer to gain a fresh perspective and be reminded that Jesus already did come as a baby in a manger to save us and will eventually come again to bring about complete restoration.

Come, Thou Long Expected Jesus

Come, Thou long expected Jesus,
Born to set Thy people free;
From our fears and sins release us;
Let us find our rest in Thee.
Israel's strength and consolation,
Hope of all the earth Thou art;
Dear Desire of ev'ry nation,
Joy of every longing heart.

Joy to those who long to see Thee
Day-spring from on high, appear.
Come, Thou promised Rod of Jesse,
Of Thy birth, we long to hear!
O'er the hills the angels singing
News, glad tidings of a birth;
"Go to Him your praises bringing
Christ the Lord has come to earth!"

Come to earth to taste our sadness,
He whose glories knew no end.
By His life He brings us gladness,
Our redeemer, Shepherd, Friend.
Leaving riches without number,
Born within a cattle stall;
This the everlasting wonder,
Christ was born the Lord of all.

Born Thy people to deliver,
Born a child, and yet a King,
Born to reign in us for ever,
Now Thy gracious kingdom bring.

By Thine own eternal Spirit
Rule in all our hearts alone;
By Thine all-sufficient merit
Raise us to Thy glorious throne.

Week 1, Day 2

COME, THOU LONG EXPECTED JESUS

On that day it will be said, "Look, this is our God; we have waited for him, and he has saved us. This is the Lord; we have waited for him. Let's rejoice and be glad in his salvation." Isaiah 25:9

It was the fall of 1981, and I had just left my friend's house having played what I believed was the most remarkable invention mankind had ever seen, the Atari 2600 gaming system. There was no question in my mind that my future happiness depended on me having one. So I waited for Christmas. During the wait, I used the opportunity to consistently give my parents solid reasons for making such an expensive request. All things considered, I argued, it was likely that it would have a positive impact on our growth as children. Only time would reveal whether they were convinced by my sound arguments. Now all I could do was wait for Christmas morning and hope for the best.

No one enjoys waiting, not even for bad news—especially not for bad news, because we'd rather know it sooner than later. Yet there are certain seasons in our lives when it seems like we are waiting indefinitely. We eagerly await the companionship of a spouse, the joy of a child, or the comfort of a place we can truly call home. We wait for the ideal job opportunity or the perfect timing to embark on our own journey. But mostly we wait on answers—answers to important questions that could determine our next stage of life, such as a job promotion to another city, lab test results, or whether that broken relationship will finally be mended. And waiting for long periods of time can lead to impatience and discouragement.

Waiting is a recurring theme in Scripture. Abraham, Sarah, Rachel, Hannah, Joseph, Moses, the Israelites, Ruth, David, and Elijah all experienced seasons of waiting. Abraham and Sarah waited for the birth of a son, just like Rachel and Hannah. Joseph waited for his circumstances to change, while Moses waited for the opportunity to lead the Israelites out of slavery. The Israelites themselves waited for forty years before they could enter the Promised Land. Ruth patiently waited for a suitable husband, while David waited for his chance to become king. Lastly, Elijah waited for the rain to come.

However, the most extended period of waiting was for the fulfillment of God's promise of a Savior, which was first mentioned in Genesis 3 and took a considerable amount of time to be fulfilled. Then God arrived in a humble manger in Bethlehem, and the angels and shepherds burst into a jubilant celebration on that very first Christmas morning. The wait was over!

I, too, burst into a joyous celebration on that Christmas morning when I discovered the game system I'd been wishing for under the tree. I couldn't help but imagine the endless enjoyment it would bring.

Waiting is hard regardless of what we're waiting for, but it's what we do in the wait that's important. Have we presented our situation to God with the unwavering faith that he is faithful regardless of the outcome? Are we aware that God frequently uses seasons of waiting to increase our dependence on him? Trust in God's providence, and you will be able to celebrate with joy no matter what happens.

Week 1, Day 3
BORN TO SET THY PEOPLE FREE

The Spirit of the Lord is on me, because he has anointed me to proclaim good news to the poor. He has sent me to proclaim freedom for the prisoners and recovery of sight for the blind, to set the oppressed free, to proclaim the year of the Lord's favor. Luke 4:18–19

Following the birth of Jesus in Bethlehem, Joseph fled to Egypt with his family and later returned to their hometown of Nazareth in Galilee after the death of King Herod. This is where Jesus spent his childhood and where he joined the townspeople every Saturday to worship in the synagogue. They knew him there as the son of Joseph and Mary. They had seen him working in the woodshop alongside his father and enjoying stickball games with other kids.

Jesus, now in his thirties, had come back to his hometown, filled with the Holy Spirit, after teaching in the synagogues across Galilee and gaining more and more popularity. No doubt the stories spreading about his ministry had made their way back to Nazareth, sparking curiosity among the locals.

On the Sabbath, he attended the synagogue, a place he would have been familiar with from his childhood. In Jewish communities, there was a long-held tradition among synagogue leaders of inviting visiting teachers to speak, so this invitation was naturally extended to Jesus. It's safe to say that his fellow townspeople would have been thrilled to have a preacher of his reputation come from their own village.

Instead of choosing any other text, Jesus deliberately selected a specific passage from the prophet Isaiah to read. It was, in fact, a famous messianic passage that the Jewish people had read for almost seven centuries. Then, after reading the text, Jesus sat down and finished by identifying himself as the one spoken of by Isaiah.

Can you picture the initial stillness that would have fallen over the audience? Then can you hear the murmuring in the room as people wondered whether Jesus was actually claiming to be the Messiah? We can imagine that they were somewhat doubtful that this man, whom they had seen grow up before their eyes, was the chosen one, born to set them free.

It's understandable when non-believers are skeptical of Jesus' proclamation of freedom since they have not yet come to know him. Fortunately, thanks to God's compassion, he never ceases to pursue them with an ongoing invitation to embrace it. However, what's more difficult to understand is the believer who has been set free yet continues to live as if they're not. It's puzzling that those that should possess the deepest understanding of Jesus also question his ability to release them from the shackles of their own limitations.

This Christmas, may you be reminded of the purpose behind the birth of the Christ child. The purpose wasn't for us to one day celebrate by singing carols, decorating trees, and exchanging gifts. Each of those elements is wonderful and adds to the joy that the season brings, but Jesus was born for a much greater mission. The purpose of his being born was to free us from the clutches of a sinful existence that ultimately leads to death. This alone should bring us an immense amount of joy and celebration! Perhaps we should start living in that freedom.

Week 1, Day 4
FROM OUR FEARS AND SINS RELEASE US

Peace I leave with you; my peace I give you. I do not give to you as the world gives. Do not let your hearts be troubled and do not be afraid. John 14:27

In Scripture, we see the evidence of two types of fear. The first is the fear of the Lord, which refers to having a deep respect, reverence, and awe for the power and authority of God. There are a couple of different ways in which this fear can manifest. For example, when we truly fear the Lord, it results in love for him, but if our fear is solely based on his wrath and anger, we will continue to live in fear of him. This latter type of fear is the appropriate reaction for an unbeliever: afraid of God's holy retribution for their sins.

However, embracing a healthy fear of the Lord brings forth many blessings and advantages. In Proverbs, Solomon is quick to point out that fearing the Lord brings wisdom, life, rest, peace, and safety and is the fountain of life.[1] I might also suggest that we could all use a little more of this type of fear.

---

1. Proverbs 1:7, 19:23, 14:26–27

Sadly, though, Christians often fall victim to another type of fear that Timothy refers to as "the spirit of fear." This type of fear can worsen because of challenging circumstances, a lack of prayer, and being isolated from other believers. Satan undoubtedly exerts extra effort to instill this fear, creating a sense of disconnection from God.

According to a survey by the American Psychological Association, 38% of people said their fear levels increase over the holidays. In short, people are grappling with a multitude of fears, from financial worries to relationship troubles, loneliness, and the general anxieties that come with the holiday season. While often depicted as a time of joy and merriment, Christmas can ironically evoke heightened feelings of anxiety and fear for many.

It's interesting to think how quickly we forget about most of our Christmas presents once the next season rolls around. However, Jesus presents us with a permanent gift. It's the gift of peace, something the world, despite its best efforts, cannot provide. At His birth, the angels declared, "Glory to God in the highest heaven, and on earth peace to those on whom his favor rests."[2] Isaiah refers to him as the Prince of Peace.[3] Through the death of Christ, we have been given the precious gift of peace that restored our relationship with God and allows our minds to be governed by peace.[4] And although we may not fully comprehend the mechanics of this peace, it still manages to bring comfort to our hearts and minds.[5]

---

2. Luke 2:14

3. Isaiah 9:6

4. Romans 5:1-2, 8:6

5. Philippians 4:7

So if, as a believer, you've been released from a spirit of fear, what do you now possess? According to Timothy, you possess a spirit characterized by power, love, and a clear, rational mind.[6] Ultimately, it's our responsibility to believe this and fully rely on God's power, putting our complete trust in Him. This carol serves as a gentle reminder that no matter what fears we face, our true peace is found in Christ. We all desire to be released from our fears, released from our sins. However, only Jesus has the power to grant us that release and offer the genuine peace our souls crave.

---

6. 2 Timothy 1:7

Week 1, Day 5
HOPE OF ALL THE EARTH THOU ART

And his name shall be the hope of the world.
Matthew 12:21

When we refer to the dictionary for a definition of hope, we find it describes it as a feeling of expectation and desire for certain things to happen. As believers, we know hope and faith are intrinsically connected. For example, the book of Hebrews teaches us that faith is being sure of what we hope for, even if we can't see it yet.[1] This type of hope is essential to our faith and based on the truth of God's Word and what he has promised us in the future.

However, we often stretch the definition of hope to include whatever desired circumstance that we want changed in our lives. And many of the things that we hope for can be wonderful things that will make our lives, or even someone else's life, better and more fulfilling. Even the Apostle Paul tells us that no one hopes for what they already have.[2]

---

1. Hebrews 11:1

2. Romans 8:24

For centuries, the Israelites had been eagerly hoping for the arrival of the promised Messiah. From the book of Genesis to Malachi, the prophets talked about the future arrival of the God of Israel as the Savior and Redeemer of the people. This is the Messianic hope that existed among the covenant people of Israel.

With the birth of Jesus, the long-awaited hope of all nations was finally realized, yet tragically, Israel failed to recognize it. You see, their hope was based on a Savior who could transform their circumstances and liberate them from Roman oppression. Put simply, they wanted a Savior who could give them the world they wanted. When Jesus boldly proclaimed himself as the long-awaited Hope, they responded with disbelief and ultimately killed him.

Christmas is a time of hope and is, in fact, the central theme of the first week of Advent. There's a pretty good chance that you're hoping for something right now. It might be worth questioning if your hope is genuinely placed in him and his promises, or if, like the Israelites, you're solely focused on wanting circumstances to change. Jesus did not come to change our circumstances. He came to change the world, beginning with the hearts and minds of each individual. And when he changes our hearts and minds, he can use us to offer hope to a broken world.

Although God has the power to change our circumstances, it's important not to rely solely on the expectation that he will. If we constantly seek better circumstances, we can easily overlook the presence of God in our everyday life. Then, in those times when our hopes don't materialize, we will find ourselves disappointed, resentful, and possibly questioning whether God truly cares. It's true that Paul hoped for something that he didn't have, to be free from the burden of whatever thorn was bothering him. While his hope didn't materialize as he had planned, he eventually discovered strength in the grace of God and became a living testament to God's power.[3] This became his new hope!

The hope we celebrate in Advent is grounded in the nature of God and the promises he has made. And true to his word, he fulfilled his promise with the arrival of Jesus into this world. If the God of the universe can make his presence known by being born a baby in a manger, then surely, he can make his presence known in any circumstance we encounter.

---

3. 2 Cor. 12:9

Week 1, Day 6
DEAR DESIRE OF EVERY NATION

> *"I will shake all nations, and they shall come to the Desire of All Nations, and I will fill this temple with glory," says the Lord of hosts.* Haggai 2:7

Picture yourself as one of the Israelite remnant who is now back in the Promised Land after being freed from Babylonian captivity. You are part of the crew responsible for completing the temple's foundation, now paving the way for construction to begin. Considering the incredible challenges you and your fellow Israelites have endured just to get this far, you should feel happy. Yet as you inspect the foundation and visualize the temple that will eventually stand on it, you become discouraged, and you're not the only one.

In fact, many people in your generation are so disheartened that they stand around weeping. This is in contrast to the younger generation, who are celebrating and dancing with joy. But you don't fault them for what they don't know. They were born during captivity and never had the chance to witness the splendor of Solomon's magnificent temple. Constructing the rest of this temple will require significant effort, and you question whether it will be worth it.

However, it isn't only that this new temple will be a poor substitute for the original. Since you were a child, you've heard stories about the dedication of the first temple, when the altar was set ablaze by heavenly fire and the entire temple was bathed in the glory of God. You think to yourself, is it even possible for that to happen now? Your heart sinks as you become more and more convinced that it likely won't happen. After all, we don't even possess the ark of the covenant anymore. What's the point?

However, your thoughts begin to change when you hear the godly words of the prophet Haggai. You're not sure if it's because he's around your same age and also remembers the grandeur of the first temple or because he possesses such an encouraging nature. After all, his name does mean, "Let's celebrate the Lord." While Haggai concedes that the new temple structure will not measure up to its predecessor, he has a message from God for us: Don't fear or be discouraged. He explains that soon God will fill this temple with a glory that will far outshine the glory of the first temple and will one day shake the world.

Even though you would never see it in your lifetime, the event unfolded centuries later exactly as Haggai had foretold. Indeed, the temple would never match the splendor of Solomon's, and there was no ark of the covenant or celestial fire illuminating the sky. Nevertheless, the temple would eventually witness an even more remarkable event when the Light of the World himself entered as a small baby. And who needed the ark of the covenant when the physical manifestation of God's Word would one day walk the courts as a man? No matter how awe-inspiring and majestic Solomon's temple had been, it could never match that!

Perhaps, similar to the Israelites, you have grown disheartened by something that you believed God was guiding you toward, but now it appears trivial. It's during moments like these that we must remind ourselves that God's capacity to perform miracles has no limits. He can turn what we consider the most insignificant things into something remarkable, such as revealing the Desire of Nations, who would one day shake the heavens and the earth.

Week 1, Day 7

JOY OF EVERY LONGING HEART

Lord, now you are letting your servant depart in peace, according to your word; for my eyes have seen your salvation. Luke 2:29–30

Perhaps you've heard the quote, "There is a God-shaped hole in the heart of each person which cannot be satisfied by any created thing but only by God the Creator." This modern paraphrase is often attributed to Blaise Pascal, a renowned writer, mathematician, scientist, and philosopher from the sixteenth century. The concept suggests that we all have a proverbial hole in our hearts, causing us to constantly yearn and search for happiness. No matter what we own, how much money we have, our health status, or the quality of our relationships, we always want more.

What's the reason behind the longing and desire that remains unfulfilled within us? According to Pascal, it was inherited from our ancestor, Adam, whose heart was designed to desire God. In fact, Adam and Eve were the only humans to ever experience genuine happiness as they strolled through the Garden of Eden, completely unaware of any kind of lack or desire. Yet the consequences of the Fall left a visible hole in the hearts of all humanity, and since then we've tried, unsuccessfully, to fill that hole by drawing from our surroundings. The problem lies in the fact that nothing created by God is intended to replace him as our ultimate desire and longing.

Unfortunately, experience is a poor teacher when it comes to desire as we never seem to learn. Time and time again, we are lured into believing that we will finally discover happiness, convinced that this time will be different, but each time we are left disappointed, drained of hope, and exhausted.

In the Gospel of Luke, we meet Simeon, a man who probably had ordinary desires and goals like other Israelite men of his time until the Holy Spirit reminded him of his mortality. There's nothing quite like a reminder of our limited time on Earth to help us zero in on what truly matters. In Simeon's case, God converted all his meaningless earthly aspirations into sheer joy as soon as he cradled the Savior of the world in his arms. From that moment on, Simeon desired nothing else and could die in peace.

How about you? Everyone's heart longs for something. If we honestly examine our motivations, we realize that all our desires ultimately lead to Christ, who is the source of true joy for every longing heart. Another famous philosopher, C.S. Lewis, once wrote, "If we find ourselves with a desire that nothing in this world can satisfy, the most probable explanation is that we were made for another world." Christ alone holds the key to that other world where you will find true and lasting fulfillment. He is the joy of every longing heart!

Week 2, Day 8
IT CAME UPON THE MIDNIGHT CLEAR—A HISTORY

At first glance, "It Came Upon the Midnight Clear" may seem like a comforting carol filled with the joyous sounds of angels singing and rejoicing over the birth of the Savior. A closer look, though, reveals a surprising and unexpected truth. Interestingly, the traditional nativity story, including the birth of Jesus, is noticeably missing from the lyrics. Could this be attributed to the fact that the author, a controversial Unitarian minister, followed a denomination that neither acknowledges the triune God nor the Incarnation of Christ? That could be one probable explanation for some of it. The more likely reason is that he was a troubled man, and his words reflected the chaotic times in which he lived. To unravel the story behind its composition, we must look to the third verse—a verse often omitted from many hymnals.

In the scenic town of Sandisfield, Massachusetts, nestled near the Berkshire Mountains, Edmund Sears was born on April 6, 1810. While sharing a childhood memory with a friend, he recounted how he used to imagine the hills reaching up to the sky, a sanctuary for radiant angels to carry out errands of love.

As the youngest of three sons of Joseph and Lucy Sears, he grew up with a father who instilled in him a deep appreciation for poetry. While juggling farm work and education, he still managed to make enough progress to be admitted as a sophomore at Union College in Schenectady, New York, in 1831. During his time there, he showcased his poetic talent and even won a contest.

After completing his education at Union, Sears worked for a short period as a lawyer and then transitioned to teaching at the Brattleboro Vermont Academy for nine months. It was here that Edmund pursued his studies for the ministry, mentored by Addison Brown, a respected minister of the Brattleboro Unitarian Church. Fascinated by the literature of Boston ministers, Edmund made the decision to attend Harvard Divinity School, hoping to follow in his mentor's footsteps and become a Unitarian minister.

Completing his studies in 1837, he began his ministry by embarking on a missionary journey to the frontier area surrounding Toledo, Ohio. He stayed there for about a year then returned to Massachusetts, where he assumed the role of pastor at the First Congregational Church and Society, a small Unitarian church in Wayland. His character and preaching left such a profound impact on the congregation that they ordained and installed him as a minister in February 1839.

After marrying Ellen Bacon that same year, Reverend Sears chose to forgo the allure of a prominent city pulpit and instead embrace tranquil country life in Wayland. However, his choice to live in a small town presented difficulties in supporting his growing family of four children. As a result, he came to realize the importance of finding a larger church that could adequately meet their needs. When the call came to serve the more prominent congregation of First Church of Christ in Lancaster, he eagerly accepted and moved on.

His decision had its drawbacks as the challenge of serving a larger church would prove too much for him, especially considering the time and circumstances in which Sears lived. The world during the late 1840s was filled with weariness and stress. The brutal Mexican–American War had just concluded the year before, leaving behind a tense atmosphere. And the American slave trade was in full swing, casting a shadow over the nation with the looming threat of civil war in the not-so-distant future. As the Industrial Revolution was gaining momentum in New England, the allure of the cities led many people to abandon their struggling farms only to face a new kind of poverty. Europe also was experiencing ongoing bloody revolutions and political unrest. Every direction he turned, there was no escape from the constant presence of violence, bloodshed, and the haunting echoes of war.

After seven years in Lancaster, Sears found himself at the lowest point in his life, feeling hopeless and depressed. The combination of these factors placed a heavy burden on Sears, and he knew he could no longer manage the responsibilities of leadership, not to mention the physical demands of a large congregation. Exhausted and near a nervous breakdown, Sears took his family and retreated back to the small town of Wayland to rest and recover until his health improved.

With Christmas approaching in 1849, Sears found solace in writing, taking advantage of his lighter workload to devote more time to it. Yet he couldn't escape what he perceived as a dark world full of sin and strife. As he started writing a poem for Christmas, his thoughts became fixated on two ideas, the first being that of a chorus of angels appearing on the night of Jesus' birth to proclaim God's message of peace on Earth and goodwill toward men. The second idea is more serious and centers on man's continual rejection of the angels' message given the persistent state of wars and conflicts worldwide.

The clearest example of this second idea is most prominently found in the poem's third verse. It's unlikely that you're as familiar with this verse as it's often excluded from many modern hymnbooks. The logic behind its omission is understandable as it delves into more weightier topics like "war," "sin and strife," and "two thousand years of wrong." It's also not set in the biblical past but focused on the dark realities of the current world in which people, like Sears, were suffering. Admittedly, these themes fall short in terms of inspiring the joyful and hopeful themes commonly associated with the Christmas season, especially with a carol that became known for congregational singing.

Sears paints a picture of a weary world filled with "sin and strife." You can almost hear his desperate plea for the world to hear the angels heralding the Christmas message. Coming from a Unitarian minister, this might seem ironic, to say the least. Unitarian theology firmly opposes the belief in the Trinity and the divinity of Christ. Their teachings emphasize Jesus was inspired, an exceptional teacher, and a role model but not considered God in human form. If there were no incarnate God, Christmas celebrations and the importance of the Christmas message would lose all significance.

This confusion and controversy led many to propose removing it from denominational hymnals altogether, though others were not so rash. Undoubtedly, Sear's poem is influenced by a specific element of the Christmas story, namely the angels delivering God's message of hope and peace as recorded in Luke 2. Noticeably missing, though, is any mention of a baby in a manger, shepherds, the wise men, or anything connected to the miraculous birth of Jesus. Some just wanted to change the carol to mention Jesus, although it's unlikely any had actually explored Sears's true convictions. Sears, in his book, *Sermons and Songs of the Christian Life* published in 1875, stated that he believed in and preached the divinity of Christ, even though he had been educated in the Unitarian denomination. It is probable that his admission resolved the matter.

Sears's poem was published the following year, in December 1850. Upon receiving it, Reverend Dr. Morrison, the editor of the *Christian Register* in Boston, Massachusetts, was so impressed with it that he showcased it in multiple Christmas programs and included it in the magazine's publication. However, the connection between the poem and the music is somewhat unclear.

Richard Storrs Willis was an American choral composer, a poet, an organist, and the brother of writer, poet, and editor Nathaniel P. Willis, a contemporary of several notable American writers, including Edgar Allan Poe and Henry Wadsworth Longfellow. He attended Yale University for his education and then pursued his passion for music by studying in Germany for six years. During this time, he had the privilege of learning under the distinguished composer Felix Mendelssohn. Willis went on to publish several books and collections of his own music. In 1850, one year after Sears composed his poem, Willis composed a tune and published under the name "Study Number 23." Later the composition would be renamed "Carol," though no one, including Willis, knows for sure who joined the text and the music.

In 1876 Willis wrote in a letter to a friend, "On my return from Europe, I found that it (the tune) had been incorporated into various church collections, apparently to Edmund Sears's text." It's worth mentioning that the poem was set to another musical arrangement as well, not just "Carol." Composer Sir Arthur Sullivan chose to use his own tune, "Noel," to set the poem to music. This melody has gained popularity and is now widely used in British hymnals. However, hymnals in the U.S. overwhelmingly prefer "Carol" by Willis.

Sears's poem conveys his profound emotions, rooted in the harsh realities of the world around him. He never could have imagined that it would go on to become one of the most beloved Christmas carols of all time. Like us, he probably saw Christmas carols as a way to share the joy of the season. His poem, on the other hand, while not devoid of hope, centered on the search for peace amid the chaos.

A Christmas poem written by a troubled man to deal with his deepest despair serves as evidence of God's ability to transform our struggles, fears, and hardships into something truly amazing. Maybe, back then, Sears couldn't imagine how his writings could be of help to anyone. But God has the power to transform the most difficult situations into a poetic masterpiece that has brought hope and peace to countless individuals worldwide for nearly two centuries. Surprisingly, Christmas presents an ideal opportunity to surrender our deepest sorrows and discover what God might unveil in our lives and the lives of others.

It Came Upon the Midnight Clear

It came upon the midnight clear,
That glorious song of old,
From angels bending near the earth
To touch their harps of gold:
"Peace on the earth, good will to men,
From heaven's all-gracious King."
The world in solemn stillness lay,
To hear the angels sing.

Still through the cloven skies they come
With peaceful wings unfurled,
And still their heavenly music floats
O'er all the weary world;
Above its sad and lowly plains,
They bend on hovering wing,
And ever o'er its Babel sounds
The blessed angels sing.

Yet with the woes of sin and strife
The world has suffered long;
Beneath the angel strain have rolled
Two thousand years of wrong;
And man, at war with man, hears not
The love-song which they bring;
Oh, hush the noise, ye men of strife
And hear the angels sing!

And ye, beneath life's crushing load,
Whose forms are bending low,
Who toil along the climbing way
With painful steps and slow,

Look now! for glad and golden hours
Come swiftly on the wing.
O rest beside the weary road,
And hear the angels sing!

For lo! the days are hastening on,
By prophet seen of old,
When with the ever-circling years
Shall come the time foretold
When peace shall over all the earth
Its ancient splendors fling,
And the whole world send back the song
Which now the angels sing.

Week 2, Day 9

IT CAME UPON THE MIDNIGHT CLEAR, THAT GLORIOUS SONG OF OLD

I consider days of old, years long past. At night I remember my music; I meditate in my heart, and my spirit ponders. **Psalm 77:5–6**

Legendary crooner Tony Bennett had a series of chart-toppers, including "Because of You," "Stranger in Paradise," and his signature song, "I Left My Heart in San Francisco." Until his passing in 2023 at the age of ninety-five, the beloved singer seemed ageless as he mesmerized audiences with his iconic performances of his classic hits well into his early nineties. Not widely known was the fact that Bennett was diagnosed with Alzheimer's disease in 2015. According to his wife, he would often seem distant or detached unless he was at the piano. Regardless of whether Tony was on stage or practicing at home, the moment the sounds of the piano keys reached his ears, he would undergo a remarkable transformation. With complete control over his extensive repertoire of songs, he would deliver unforgettable hour-and-a-half performances.

Neuroscientists suggest that when we actively engage in performing or singing music, as opposed to simply listening to it, we tap into our "procedural" memory, which is an unconscious mechanism for remembering daily habits and routines. Typically, Alzheimer's affects other areas of memory before impacting the ability to remember lyrics and perform, which is why individuals with dementia often retain these skills.

One doesn't necessarily have to be a neuroscientist to recognize that music can provoke strong emotions and trigger nostalgic memories from years ago. It's incredible how we can't remember what we just jotted down on a grocery list but can easily recollect the lyrics of a song from many years ago and be instantly transported to that moment.

Close your eyes and let yourself drift back in time, exploring if there are any particular memories connected to this carol. Allow yourself to be transported to that moment, reliving the emotions and experiences that are forever intertwined. Maybe it reminds you of a particular church service, singing carols, or a festive family get-together. For me, it takes me back over forty years to hear the nostalgic sound of my mom's Andy Williams album playing on the vintage stereo in the cozy corner of our living room.

What is the true message that the "glorious song of old" urges us to remember? In a stunning display, the God of the universe broke through time and space, forsaking his glorious throne to be born as a humble baby to poor peasants in a stable. That same baby would one day grow up and give his life on a cruel cross to save humanity before finally ascending to his rightful position at his Father's side in heaven, beckoning us all to come to him. That sounds like a glorious song worth remembering.

Week 2, Day 10
PEACE ON EARTH, GOOD WILL TO MEN, FROM HEAVEN'S ALL-GRACIOUS KING

Glory to God in the highest, And on earth peace, goodwill toward men! Luke 2:14

In his famous poem, Edmund Sears pleads with people to hear the angels' message for peace on Earth, stressing the critical nature of the situation. The world he lived in was filled with never-ending conflict, and it weighed heavily on him, affecting his ability to find inner peace. It was reasonable for Sears to desire peaceful resolutions to the problems that he observed affecting both the world and his personal life. Our own chaotic world is filled with a constant stream of negative news updates that serve as a grim reminder of the absence of peace.

Maybe this Christmas season has left you longing for inner peace, feeling uncertain and afraid about something that appears beyond your control. It's possible that you're struggling to find a resolution to interpersonal conflicts with loved ones, friends, or colleagues. Additionally, when you consider the chaos in your local community, the nation, and the world at large, it becomes clearer why Sears implores everyone to awaken to the angel's message.

What if we approached the angel's message of peace on Earth from a different perspective? Rather than prioritizing peace in our lives, relationships, and the world, we redirect our primary emphasis to finding peace through our relationship with God. In Scripture, Paul clearly indicates that our natural human condition is to be at war with God.[1] To put it differently, we were God's enemy, trapped in a battle with no chance of victory and nothing to offer him to resolve the conflict. There was no neutral ground. It was a hopeless situation.

And then, out of nowhere, something quite unusual occurred. The unmistakable Victor came forward to reconcile the relationship with an offering of peace. Peace would be provided to us, the losing party, without any cost on our part. However, the conquering King would have to pay a heavy price as it would require the sacrifice of his own Son. The giving of the Son was itself the message of peace the angels were referring to. None of us would ever consider making such a precious peace offering with our own enemy.

We all desire peace from whatever internal or external conflicts keep us up at night. Yet our most pressing need is for peace with God. Above all, Jesus' primary purpose on Earth was to reconcile God with disobedient and sinful human beings. The true peace we all desperately need is everlasting, unlike the temporary peace we desire in other aspects of our lives.

Does this imply that we should abandon our quest for peace in other areas of life? Absolutely not! Nevertheless, we should keep in mind that the extent of peace we experience will fluctuate as long as we live in this world. Jesus predicted we would en-

---

1. Romans 8:7

counter trouble and persecution during our time on Earth, but he also told us not to be troubled or afraid, because the peace he offers differs from what the world offers. When we embrace his offer of peace, it opens the door for peace to flow into other areas of our lives. With the Holy Spirit as our guide, we can attain a sense of inner peace and strive to maintain peaceful interactions with others to the extent that it is within our power.

Week 2, Day 11
STILL THROUGH THE CLOVEN SKIES THEY COME WITH PEACEFUL WINGS UNFURLED

Then an angel of the Lord stood before them, and the glory of the Lord shone around them, and they were terrified. Luke 2:9

The Christmas classic, *It's a Wonderful Life*, tells the story of small-town businessman George Bailey, who, because of circumstances beyond his control, is on the brink of losing everything and is contemplating taking his own life. Just as he is about to carry out his plan, Clarence, his guardian angel, swoops in and shows George a glimpse of a world where he never existed. The movie is a beloved tradition during the holiday season, especially for those who, like myself, eagerly anticipate the sound of the bell ringing, signifying Clarence's well-deserved wings.

However, it's clear that the movie takes a creative approach, straying far from the words of Scripture. In the film, the angel, Clarence, is portrayed as a man who has passed away and is now an angel second class eagerly awaiting his chance to earn his wings. Naturally, we understand that when people pass away, their aspiration is to become saints, not angels. Second, if Clarence succeeds in showing George the beauty and significance of life, he will finally earn his wings. This, too, is not biblical.

The Greek word for angel in the Bible, "angelos," is a word that simply means messenger. When it comes to angels, the image that has become widely accepted and popularized through various forms of art, stories, and modern media is essentially that of a human with wings. According to the book of Hebrews, angels are described as spiritual beings with no necessarily physical form. Angels do, however, possess the ability to take on human form and have done so many times in the Bible. For instance, Abraham had a meal in the company of angels, and Daniel, Zechariah, and Mary all received visits from the angel Gabriel.[1] It's important to note that in all these instances, the angels are never depicted as winged creatures.

Even in today's text, the angel of the Lord is described as standing before the shepherds. Before you go tearing the wings off the angels in your nativity set, angels are sometimes described as having wings. For example, the cherubim on the ark of the covenant had wings, and Isaiah and Ezekiel both had visions of angels with wings.[2]

You might be questioning the significance given that you've never seen an angel, with or without wings. Before you hastily jump to that conclusion, pause for a moment, and reflect on the timeless advice from Hebrews. It reminds us to show kindness to strangers, for we may unknowingly encounter angels in our

---

1. Luke 1:19, 26; Daniel 9:21

2. Exodus 25:20, Ezekiel 1, Isaiah 6:1–2

daily lives.[3] Keep this thought in mind this Christmas as you navigate through crowded stores, interact with busy salesclerks, and share the road with your fellow drivers. When you live with the expectation that every interaction has the potential to introduce unexpected heavenly beings, you will infuse your everyday life with a sense of wonder.

---

3. Hebrews 13:2

Week 2, Day 12
O REST BESIDE THE WEARY ROAD AND HEAR THE ANGELS SING!

Come to me, all you who are weary and burdened, and I will give you rest. Matthew 11:28

Have you ever paused to consider the background and circumstances surrounding this particular statement by Jesus? One possible understanding of this verse is that Jesus promises to ease our burdens and bring us a life of peace and restfulness if we faithfully follow him. While there may be some truth to that statement, it's important to thoroughly examine the entire passage in order to fully comprehend it.

Jesus, having empowered the twelve disciples to cast out demons and heal diseases, embarked on his own missionary journey, preaching and teaching across the towns of Galilee. He spent a considerable amount of time working in the Galilean towns of Bethsaida, Chorazin, and Capernaum only to condemn them later for their lack of repentance. He drew a comparison between their towns and the ancient Gentile cities of Tyre, Sidon, and Sodom. The Jews living in those Galilean towns would have found this comparison highly offensive, believing that they were certainly not as morally corrupt as the cities they were being compared to.

This was specifically what Jesus aimed to convey. Had any of those morally corrupt Gentile cities been fortunate enough to witness the ministry of Jesus, they would have repented without hesitation. But since these Galilean towns had both heard of him and been a witness to his miracles and then consciously and deliberately rejected him, they would suffer a more severe judgment than the Gentile towns that had never heard of him. They stubbornly held on to their own useless knowledge and arrogance, feeling secure and satisfied with their own achievements in life. And instead of recognizing their need for a Messiah to set them free, they chose to burden themselves with the impossible task of obeying written laws they could not keep.

As Christmas approaches, take the time to consider if your life is beginning to resemble those who lived in Bethsaida, Chorazin, and Capernaum. Are you stubbornly refusing to acknowledge your own burdens and rejecting the help of Jesus, thinking you have everything under control? Are you attempting to find rest through your possessions, wealth, authority, connections, knowledge, or social standing? Maybe you're on the opposite side of the spectrum, pointing fingers at others for your heavy load.

If we're truly honest with ourselves, we'll admit that all of our own efforts weigh us down and fill us with a sense of restlessness. Jesus draws a parallel between this feeling and a lack of faith. He claims that knowing him is the only way to truly understand the meaning of rest. Come to me; I'll give you rest. Come to me; I'll reveal the Father to you. Jesus is extending the invitation to you too. You're invited to come to him and submit all of your burdens to him with the promise that if you accept the invitation, he will give you rest.

Week 2, Day 13
YET WITH THE WOES OF SIN AND STRIFE THE WORLD HAS SUFFERED LONG

We know that all creation has been groaning with the pains of childbirth up to the present time. Romans 8:22

When we were kids, we eagerly looked forward to Christmas, envisioning the twinkling lights, the sound of carols playing in the stores, and the scent of freshly baked cookies, all filling us with happiness and anticipation. That same type of eager anticipation is at the heart of what Advent represents: faithful believers of Christ gathering to celebrate his initial advent into this world as a humble baby while eagerly awaiting his second coming to reconcile heaven and Earth.

Perhaps at this point, you have some concerns. Although you eagerly await the celebration of Christ's initial arrival through Christmas every year, you question whether you're anxiously awaiting his second coming. You don't have to worry, because according to the apostle Paul, you're actually longing for the return of Christ, whether you realize it or not.

Using the metaphor of "creation groaning," Paul explains that since sin entered the world, there has been a clear and ongoing groaning from all creation as it longs to be free from the bondage of sin and death. The impact of sin on your own life, whether self-inflicted or the result of living in a fallen world, cannot be denied. Anytime your body groans out of struggles, suffering, and pain is proof that it yearns for something different. That something different is to be freed once and for all from all the groaning.

Paul goes on to employ another powerful metaphor, likening the groaning to the weariness of a pregnant woman nearing her due date. Jesus had used this same analogy of childbirth to illustrate the temporary nature of suffering.[1] In other words, while there's no question that the pain is intense and real, it's a precursor to the joyous moment of childbirth, after which all the pain will vanish.

In this passage, Paul isn't ignoring or dismissing human suffering. If anything, he's emphasizing the reality of suffering and helping you understand why you deeply "groan" for something better. Pain is an unpleasant but unavoidable part of life. Like a woman in labor that endures the pain for the eventual happiness it brings, we, too, should maintain hope and practice patience, trusting that God will use our pain and suffering for his greater good.[2]

This is why during Christmas, you can experience the happiness of God's light entering the world even while you simultaneously feel the heaviness of the darkness that exists in the world. Yet those that possess faith anticipate the arrival of something greater, firmly holding onto the belief that darkness

---

1. John 16:21–22

2. Romans 8:28

and pain will not have the final say. The world's renovation and humanity's redemption will be the final word, a prospect that we can eagerly look forward to!

Week 2, Day 14

OH, HUSH THE NOISE, YE MEN OF STRIFE AND HEAR THE ANGELS SING

> *Stop fighting, and know that I am God, exalted among the nations, exalted on the earth.* Psalm 46:10

Many of you may be familiar with this verse, which is more commonly translated, "Be still and know that I am God." The idea being that unless we find moments of silence, we will not be able to hear from God, as His voice gets drowned out amidst the noise and restlessness of our lives. Although this advice is priceless during the chaotic holiday season, I urge you to take a moment and immerse yourself in the impactful words of all eleven verses of Psalm 46. When you do, you will uncover something even more remarkable.

The psalmist begins by vividly portraying some of the most awe-inspiring and humbling natural phenomena imaginable. Those who have experienced hurricanes, earthquakes, and tornadoes understand the immense power and destruction that nature can unleash. But through it all, we are commanded not to fear, because God's greatness exceeds all natural occurrences.

The psalmist then turns his attention to man-made problems, like the political instability in the world, which include wars and the downfall of nations. It was amid a distressing situation like this that Edmund Sears penned his Christmas poem, capturing the raw emotions and turmoil of his time. And today, the continuous news cycle we find ourselves in makes it increasingly difficult to escape feelings of worry and stress brought on by the constant presence of violence, bloodshed, and reminders of war around the world.

Strangely, in this instance, God does not provide the usual command: do not fear. The Hebrew term "rapha" in verse ten has multiple interpretations such as "be still," "let go," "release," or "stop." Considering the battle implications of verse nine, I appreciate the way the Christian Standard Bible interprets God's command for us to "stop fighting" in verse ten. But there's a reason that we are to stop fighting, and that reason is to gain knowledge—but knowledge about what, specifically?

The 46th Psalm serves as a powerful reminder that there are aspects of life that we simply cannot control. Just like we can't control peace around the world, we also can't control the unpredictable forces of nature. But fortunately for us, we know someone who can! Once we let go of our fears and stop fighting a losing battle, we can find peace in the knowledge that God is fully in control of this world and has already won the battle. That knowledge, even though it reminds of us of our limitations, delivers freedom from the stress and anxiety that it might otherwise bring.

With the New Year just around the corner, why not make a resolution to stop fearing and fighting against the things you cannot control? Then dedicate yourself daily to increasing your knowledge of God who is in complete control.

Week 3, Day 15

WHAT CHILD IS THIS?—A HISTORY

Picture the combination of a Scottish insurance salesman, crippling depression that confines him to his bed, and a well-known sixteenth century English folk tune that revolves around a woman, perhaps with a scandalous reputation, wearing green sleeves. Would such a fusion give birth to a treasured Christmas carol heard in countless churches for over 150 years? Likely not! Yet the remarkable story behind "What Child Is This?" serves as a poignant reminder that God can use the challenges faced by ordinary people, combined with unexpected resources, to capture the wonder and mystery of the greatest moment in human history.

It's rare to come across a hymn from nineteenth century England that wasn't penned by a minister. William Chatterton Dix was that notable exception. Dix was born in Bristol, England, to Susannah and John Ross Dix in 1837. Besides being a well-respected surgeon, his father was also a prolific writer who published brief biographies of notable figures in literature, ministry, and politics. He even dedicated one entire book to his favorite English poet, Thomas Chatterton. William Dix was given his middle name in tribute to the poet.

As Dix grew up, he, too, developed a love for literature, influenced by his father's affection for poetry. He received training in the liberal arts, but his education at the Bristol Grammar School focused on grooming him for a career in business. And though he did not become a doctor like his father, he followed in his father's footsteps and pursued writing as a source of joy rather than a source of income.

Upon finishing his education, he secured a managerial role at a marine insurance company in Glasgow, Scotland. He found satisfaction in maintaining a regular lifestyle while closing large insurance deals. Even though Dix was a driven and accomplished insurance professional, his true love for poetry emerged most prominently when he fell ill.

In 1865, when Dix was only twenty-nine years old, he was struck by a severe and nearly fatal illness that left him bedridden for an extended period. This unexpected setback was a devastating blow to a successful young man full of energy in his twenties. As his body fought for survival, he found himself confined to his bed day after day, feeling the weight of the battle. Sadly, even after the worst had passed, he was left with a considerable amount of time left to recover, leading him to spiral into a deep depression.

Through the healing process, Dix experienced a spiritual awakening that ignited his poetic spirit and inspired him to pursue writing. Over time, he discovered not only healing for his physical and mental needs but also a profound spiritual connection with God. He emerged from the crisis as a man of unwavering faith, a dedicated prayer warrior, and an avid reader of the Bible, incorporating Christian themes into his poetry.

During this healing journey, he channeled his thoughts and feelings into a lengthy poem entitled "The Manger Throne." From this inspiring poem, he extracted three verses, which became the lyrics to "What Child Is This?" This carol stands out from others because it offers a unique viewpoint, presenting a confused onlooker at the manger questioning the identity of the newborn baby. What compels angels to sing, shepherds to

WEEK 3, DAY 15   51

watch, and kings to bring gifts to a baby lying in a manger in such harsh circumstances? The response would come as a joyful proclamation of the baby's divine nature—that he is Christ the King!

After recovering from his illness, Dix went back to work but also continued writing. While many of his poems remained unseen, there was one that Dix held close to his heart and felt compelled to share with others. There's no evidence to suggest that Dix had any musical ability, and it remains unclear if he even considered his poem suitable for musical adaptation. Nevertheless, in 1871, six years after its origin, the poem earned a place of honor in the influential collection of carols known as *Christmas Carols Old and New* in the United Kingdom.

While it's not known with certainty who paired the three stanzas of Dix's poem with music, it's widely believed that Sir John Stainer, the hymnal editor and composer, was responsible for harmonizing the musical setting. Stainer searched for a melody that would give the poem a sense of grandeur and significance. However, the arrangement he selected turned out to be an interesting, if not unusual, choice of a folk song that had existed for three centuries.

As the story goes, the year was 1580 when a man named Richard Jones unknowingly made history at the London Stationer's Company. He became the first person to register a song with lyrics that told a tale of a lady adorned in green sleeves. The song was titled "A Newe Northen Dittye of ye Ladye Greene Sleves." Although his lyrics were not religious or particularly respectable, the "lady in green sleeves" concept became very popular. Suddenly everyone had a "green sleeves" tune, and license application associated with the melody exploded at the Stationer's Company in the same year.

In 1584 the tune found its place in the book, *A Handful of Pleasant Delights*, where it was more popularly known as

"A New Courtly Sonnet of the Lady Green Sleeves." Shakespeare went on to add to the melody's fame by featuring "Greensleeves" two times in his play, *The Merry Wives of Windsor*, in 1597. The somber melody was played in the background by hired musicians while traitors were hanged.

Some argue the melody is considerably older. According to popular legend, Henry VIII is credited with writing it for his lover, Anne Boleyn, after she rejected his advances. This would have occurred approximately seventy years prior to when the song was first registered in print. However, this fascinating story is likely a legend, as the musical style bears a stronger resemblance to the Italian compositional style that arrived in England after Henry's passing. It's widely believed that the song originated during the reign of Queen Elizabeth as she was often seen dancing to it.

While the early history of the folk tune is shrouded in mystery, "Greensleeves" became a well-known drinking song in pubs, with lyrics that were quite scandalous. The song's lyrics revolve around a rejected lover accusing Lady Greensleeves of rudely abandoning him. This is despite the fact that he showered her with love; paid for her accommodations; and gave her a petticoat, an embellished gown, and a necklace adorned with jewels. Back then, wearing a "green gown" was seen as a sign of promiscuity. This term referred to a dress that had grass stains on it, which suggested engaging in intimate activities outside. Many speculate that the "lady green sleeves" described in the song may have been a prostitute.

Why did Stainer, more than three hundred years later, incorporate an old folk song, possibly about a prostitute, into a carol that celebrates the birth of Jesus? The melody itself is a bit out of the ordinary for a Christmas song as it's written in a minor key, creating a sense of melancholy. Interestingly, it appears that Stainer wasn't the first to associate this tune with Christmas. In the 1640s, the tune was paired with another ancient Christmas-themed poem known as "The Old Year Now Away Is Fled." This particular carol was very popular in its time and was sung for hundreds of years before Stainer took his own gamble with the melody. However, the risk seemed to be worth it as the disreputable folk tune, now with its revised lyrics, became one of the most cherished Christmas carols ever. Today it's performed in churches all over the world, with most people completely unaware of its controversial beginnings.

It's important to mention that William Chatterton Dix was not a pastor, missionary, or theologian, nor did he make any claims to be. He worked as an insurance salesman, waking up every day to go to his office and sell insurance policies to those that required them. All accounts indicate that he dedicated himself to his work and excelled in his chosen profession, continuing to sell insurance policies until his passing in 1898 at the age of sixty-one. Yet throughout his lifetime, he would go on to compose over forty notable hymns, including "As with Gladness, Men of Old," "Alleluia! Sing to Jesus," and many more.

We often make the mistake of believing that our current situation, background, profession, or upbringing make us unsuitable to be used by God. We might even question what kind of influence our normal, everyday life can have in sharing our faith. In such moments, it's crucial to remember the impact of William Chatterton Dix, an ordinary individual who went to work every day selling insurance policies that have long since been forgotten but whose poem of praise still resonates with us today.

What Child Is This?

What Child is this, who, laid to rest,
On Mary's lap is sleeping?
Whom angels greet with anthems sweet,
While shepherds watch are keeping?

Chorus:
This, this is Christ, the King,
Whom shepherds guard and angels sing:
Haste, haste to bring Him laud,
The Babe, the Son of Mary!

Why lies He in such mean estate,
Where ox and ass are feeding?
Good Christian, fear: for sinners here
The silent Word is pleading.

So bring Him incense, gold, and myrrh,
Come, peasant, king to own Him.
The King of kings salvation brings;
Let loving hearts enthrone Him.

What Child Is This? – William Chatterton Dix Version

What child is this, who, laid to rest
On Mary's lap, is sleeping?
Whom angels greet with anthems sweet
While shepherds watch are keeping?

This, this is Christ the King,
Whom shepherds guard and angels sing;
Haste, haste to bring him laud,
The babe, the son of Mary.

Why lies he in such mean estate
Where ox and ass are feeding?
Good Christian, fear: for sinners here
The silent Word is pleading.

Nails, spear shall pierce him through,
The cross be borne for me, for you.
Hail, hail the Word made flesh,
The babe, the son of Mary.

So bring him incense, gold, and myrrh,
Come, peasant, king, to own him;
The King of kings salvation brings,
Let loving hearts enthrone him.

Raise, raise a song on high,
The virgin sings her lullaby.
Joy, joy, for Christ is born,
The babe, the son of Mary.

Week 3, Day 16
WHAT CHILD IS THIS, WHO, LAID TO REST

He asked them, "But who do you say I am?"
Matthew 16:15

They often had private conversations with their master, and this was one such occasion. Though they enjoyed these discussions, they often found them to be quite challenging. Jesus tended to speak in parables or riddles, leaving them feeling puzzled and confused. However, today was not one of those days. He spoke with clarity, and his words were direct. He simply asked them, "Who do people say I am?"

Whew! The question was so easy that each disciple eagerly jumped in with their answer. Actually, they wondered if it was a trick question since rumors about Jesus' true identity were the main subject of most conversations in the Galilean countryside. Surely he must have heard some of the rumors floating around considering the incredible acts he was performing. You can't heal the sick and lame, restore sight to the blind, and miraculously feed thousands of people without questions starting to circulate. The religious leaders, upon hearing about Jesus' actions and teachings, also wished for him to prove his identity and perform a miracle for their own benefit. Even King Herod had questions, his mind racing with thoughts of his old rival, John the Baptist, wondering if he had returned from the dead.

Each disciple, desperate to impress Jesus with their answer, began vying for his attention by talking over one another. "Some say you are John the Baptist, others Elijah, and still others say that one of the prophets from long ago has come back to life." Then they all sat back, exchanging satisfied nods and feeling a surge of confidence while thinking, *You're welcome, Jesus! If you have more questions, please do not hesitate to ask.* Coincidentally, Jesus did have another question for each of them that was waiting to be answered. "But what about you?" he questioned, examining the eyes of each disciple before him. "Who do you say that I am?"

The group fell silent, and their confident smiles disappeared. They all looked at each other, waiting for someone to speak, and most turned their attention to Peter. Without fail, he was always the first to speak up. Hopefully he wouldn't let them down this time. Taking a deep breath, Peter's voice gained intensity as he proclaimed, "You are the Messiah, the Son of the living God!"

Most people would let that kind of fame go to their heads—everyone wondering who they are. But not Jesus. He rather thought it was irrelevant. The real question on his mind was who the disciples thought he was.

William Chatterton Dix was confronted with that question while lying in his sickbed: Who exactly is this child that was born in Bethlehem some two thousand years ago? Is Jesus simply considered a prophet or miracle worker confined to the annals of history? Or does his birth point to something much more?

It's ironic that a large part of the world will observe Christmas this year without a true understanding of who this Jesus is that they are celebrating. What about you? Who do you say this baby in a manger was? Moreover, do you have the courage, like Peter, to boldly declare that you know who he is and then confidently spread that message to others this Christmas?

Week 3, Day 17
THIS, THIS IS CHRIST THE KING

For there is born to you this day in the city of David a Savior, who is Christ the Lord. Luke 2:11

Whenever I meet someone, I have this terrible habit of immediately thinking about what I'm going to say next. As a result, I often end up forgetting their name, even though they just told me. Had I been a humble shepherd that incredible night when a multitude of angels appeared to announce the birth of Jesus, this flaw would have led to immense problems. Amid all the excitement, I surely would have regretted not having something to jot down notes, because the angel of the Lord never actually tells us the child's name but instead reveals who he is.

The angel's first identifying feature of the baby that had been born was that he was the Savior. What is a savior? Merriam-Webster defines savior as one that saves from danger or destruction. In that context, what peril does the angel imply we need saving from? Joseph received the answer to this dilemma from another divine messenger while pondering how to handle his pregnant fiancée. Joseph was told by that angel to give the baby being born to Mary the name Jesus, as he would save people from their sins.[1] In all likelihood, the Jews during that time believed Roman occupation was their most urgent issue to be saved from. But it wasn't. Sin was their greatest problem, for which there was no remedy until now.

Next the angel identified the baby as Christ. The term "Christ" originates from the Greek word "Christos," which translates to "anointed one" or "chosen one." It can also be translated as "Messiah." Throughout the Old Testament, prophecies foretold of a future king who would come from the lineage of David. This king would rule over Israel with unwavering justice and righteousness for all eternity. The title "Christ" signifies that He is the chosen one of God, the fulfillment of the Old Testament prophecies, who will usher in the peace that the world needs.

Finally, the angel identifies the baby as Lord. Once again, according to Merriam-Webster, the term "Lord" refers to one having power and authority over others. When the angel referred to Jesus as Lord, there was an unmistakable implication of the divine. Put simply, this Savior, this Messiah, that Joseph was to name Jesus, was God himself.

The angel's proclamation of this baby's identity is truly shocking, but sometimes we fail to fully grasp its magnitude amid all the holiday commotion. Take a moment to stop and carefully consider it. This baby that was born to a humble peasant couple in Bethlehem and was lying in a feeding trough was the very incarnation of God himself! Furthermore, the angels proclaimed that he arrived with a purpose. He has come to be our Savior, rescuing us from the burden of our sins. He has come to be our long-awaited King, the Messiah, who brings an eternal reign and endless peace. And he has come to be the Lord over our lives with complete authority over both heaven and Earth.

---

1. Matthew 1:21

While it would have been useful information for the shepherds to know Jesus' name that evening, it was the profound realization of his true nature that would forever transform their lives and ours.

Week 3, Day 18
WHY LIES HE IN SUCH MEAN ESTATE

She gave birth to her firstborn son. She wrapped him in strips of cloth and laid him in a manger because there wasn't any room for them in the inn.
Luke 2:7

We all love an underdog story, and that's exactly why the movie, *Cinderella Man*, is one of my favorites. This film portrays the real-life journey of James Braddock, a boxer who defied all odds during the Great Depression by returning to the ring and ultimately becoming the heavyweight champion of the world. At a time when America desperately needed a savior, an unlikely hero stepped forward, showcasing the incredible resilience and determination to secure a fresh start for his family and himself.

The earthly life of Jesus Christ certainly didn't start out in the most ideal conditions either. He was born into poverty in a small, cramped stable filled with the smell of animals and the sound of their rustling. But even before his birth, his mother, Mary, faced the threat of severe repercussions for being pregnant, including the possibility of being stoned. Luckily her fiancé, Joseph, a local carpenter, would intervene to prevent that from occurring. However, this undoubtedly led to tensions within their extended family, societal scorn, and potential damage to his business.

Despite their poverty, the couple's unwavering dedication to each other was rooted in their commitment to following God's plan for their lives. But there must have been a moment when Joseph questioned the wisdom of this plan, knowing that he had to undertake a dangerous ninety-mile trip to Bethlehem with his pregnant wife, who was ready to deliver at any moment. When they finally reached Bethlehem, their relief was short lived as they discovered that there were no accommodations available. They had no choice but to make do with a cave, where Mary would soon give birth. After the baby was born, they laid their baby in a dirty and smelly feeding trough that animals had used.

Regrettably, the arrival of Jesus did not bring an end to their troubles either. Joseph soon received a warning in a dream about King Herod's intentions to harm the baby, prompting him to swiftly gather his young family and escape to Egypt. It would be years before they were finally able to return home to Nazareth. From the very beginning, Jesus faced many challenges and disadvantages, making his story the epitome of an underdog. And he is the Son of God!

Unfortunately, playing the victim card has become all too common in our culture. We attribute our problems to factors such as our social status, financial situation, upbringing, influence, cultural background, and other causes. Jesus never played the victim card despite having all the circumstances that could have led him to do so. Actually, on the night he was arrested, he reassured his disciples not to be concerned because he had already conquered the world. Jesus was already claiming victory before the Resurrection had even occurred!

Perhaps you're thinking that of course he could claim victory. He is, after all, God in the flesh. But really, why should that concern us? Sure, Jesus had an advantage, but let's not overlook the fact that we, as believers, have our own advantage too! The Spirit of Jesus lives inside each of us, allowing us to do all things through Christ, who gives us strength. According to the apostle Paul, we are not only conquerors but also eternally connected to God's love. That should give us confidence right there!

This Christmas, instead of making excuses, it might be the perfect opportunity to take responsibility for something you've been avoiding. Be the underdog in your own story, whom God empowers to achieve something remarkable for his glory.

Week 3, Day 19
THE SILENT WORD IS PLEADING

After the earthquake there was a fire. But the Lord wasn't in the fire. And after the fire there was a quiet, whispering voice. 1 Kings 19:12

It's fascinating how cultural terms like "grinch" have seamlessly made their way into our everyday language. For example, if you happen to express any dissatisfaction with Christmas, you're quickly branded as a grinch. Grinch, in this case, refers to the beloved 1966 animated Christmas classic, *How the Grinch Stole Christmas!* Those of us who grew up watching *The Grinch* every year, as well as the popular movie adaptation, are familiar with the story of the small-hearted Grinch, who despised Christmas to such an extent that he desired to bring misery upon all the Whos in Who-ville.

The Grinch was convinced that he needed to devise a plan to prevent Christmas from arriving. His primary concern was the noise associated with Christmas. "For, tomorrow, I know all the Who girls and boys will wake bright and early," said the Grinch. "They'll rush for their toys! And then! Oh, the noise! Oh, the noise! Noise! Noise! Noise! There's one thing I hate! All the NOISE! NOISE! NOISE! NOISE!"

The Grinch is definitely on to something when it comes to the excessive noise during the Christmas season. Sure, there are the normal sounds of children joyfully playing with their toys on Christmas morning, but honestly, those are not the sounds that are most distracting. No doubt, as you read these words, Christmas-themed advertisements surround you, constantly reminding you to indulge in holiday shopping. Everywhere you go, holiday music fills the air, streaming from speakers in your house, car, malls, and stores. And then there are the social events and family get-togethers filled with lively conversations and packed with people. Even the church is involved in adding to the noise of Christmas. Don't forget the Christmas plays, musicals to enjoy, and, oh yes, carols to sing.

And yet...throughout it all, the silent Word is pleading. Pleading for a few silent moments where you can reflect on God's Word long enough to hear the very presence of God.

The prophet Elijah received a command from God to make his way to a mountain and get ready to experience the Lord's presence. The mountain trembled as a strong and forceful wind ripped through, causing rocks to shatter, but the Lord's presence was not found in the wind. Both an earthquake and a fire followed, but the Lord was not present in either of them. But then, after the fire, a profound silence settled in, and Elijah heard a quiet, whispering voice.

Scripture clearly documents instances when God acted in dramatic ways. Consider the book of Acts, where on the day of Pentecost, the disciples were visited by the Holy Spirit, who arrived like a forceful wind and manifested as tongues of fire. However, this is not the usual way God interacts with us in our daily lives. We are most likely to hear God's voice when we become still and calm. Like Jesus, who often retreated to peaceful spots away from the bustling crowds, we, too, should find quiet places to commune with our heavenly Father.

In the midst of the noise that surrounds you this Christmas, perhaps the silent Word is pleading for you to slow down and listen. There is no question that the Lord has something important to convey to you. The real question is, will you listen to his pleas?

Week 3, Day 20

SO BRING HIM INCENSE, GOLD, AND MYRRH

When they entered the house, they saw the child with his mother Mary. So they bowed down and worshiped him. Then they opened their treasure chests and offered him gifts of gold, frankincense, and myrrh. Matthew 2:11

Imagine for a moment that you're Mary, the mother of Jesus. The day is unfolding like countless others before, with routine tasks and familiar sights. As you work outside doing chores, you can feel the warmth of the sun on your skin while your toddler son, Jesus, plays happily nearby. From a distance, you catch sight of a group of impeccably dressed men exuding an air of opulence while their entourage trails behind them. Without giving it much thought, you continue with your work, dismissing the significance of the situation. When you glance up once more, it dawns on you that they are making their way toward your home. Even though they appear harmless, you feel uneasy and call out to Joseph, who is working nearby, before taking Jesus safely inside your home.

The sound of Joseph's voice talking with the men drifts in from outside, his tone steady and composed, easing any concerns you may have had. However, you cannot make out what they are discussing. Then the door slowly creaks open, and Joseph walks through with a look of astonishment on his face, followed by a group of lavishly dressed men. As their gaze meets yours, the men's eyes quickly shift to the child standing next to you, their faces reflecting a powerful combination of emotion and awe.

As a mother, your instincts kick in, urging you to reach out and pull Jesus close for protection, yet you pause, unsure of the cause of your hesitation. Then, in a breathtaking moment, these wealthy and powerful men drop to their knees and bow before your son, their voices filled with adoration and praise. As you look to your husband for an answer, you can see the same mixture of amazement and bewilderment in his eyes.

It isn't the first time that something similar has happened, yet you remain in awe every time. Right after giving birth to Jesus, a group of shepherds, their clothes smelling of sheep, gathered in your makeshift birthing room, which happened to be a stable for animals, in order to worship him. Amazingly, they claimed to have been sent by angels! Then, when you and Joseph took Jesus to the temple for his dedication, an old prophetess named Anna and a kind older gentleman named Simeon sought you out to praise God for your son. You take a deep breath and wonder if it will always be this way.

While the men's voices echo in praise of Jesus, their entourage enters, bearing gifts of gold, incense, and myrrh, which they reverently place before him. As you stare at the lavish gifts, you can't help but ponder their value, realizing that Joseph will never accumulate such wealth in his entire life. Then, as quickly as they came, the men depart but with an unmistakable sense of joy in their hearts. It is clear that they have finally found in your son what they have been seeking for a long time.

When it comes to the story of the magi, our tendency is to primarily view it from the magi's point of view. However, there's no doubt that Mary was there, and it's reasonable to assume that Joseph was also present. While Scripture remains silent on the specifics of the event's unfolding or Mary's reaction, I can't help but imagine it happened similarly.

Even today, in a culture and age where following Jesus is often deemed foolish, we, too, should be in awe when the wise, wealthy, and influential humble themselves before him and offer their treasures in worship. It's the proper response for anyone who encounters King Jesus.

Week 3, Day 21
THE KING OF KINGS, SALVATION BRINGS

He will be great and will be called the Son of the Most High, and the Lord God will give him the throne of his father David. He will reign over the house of Jacob forever, and his kingdom will have no end. Luke 1:32–33

In 1380 King Charles VI of France took the throne when he was just eleven years old and remained in power for forty-two years. His rule was marked by ongoing battles with England and internal conflicts within his own kingdom. When he died, the Duke of Uzès, a prominent French nobleman, understood the high stakes involved with various influential factions competing for control of the monarchy. Hence, the moment the king's casket was lowered into the vault of the Basilica of Saint-Denis in northern Paris, the duke loudly proclaimed, "The king is dead. Long live the king!"

This seemingly contradictory phrase, which is the first known public declaration of it, leaves us wondering what the duke actually meant. Well, it seems he was making every effort to prevent a succession crisis. When there is no clear successor to the throne and the line of succession is uncertain, it can trigger a crisis that plunges the country into civil war. So the expression, "the king is dead," means that the current ruler has died, and "long live the king" expresses support for the new monarch who immediately succeeds his predecessor. In this case, it was the king's son, King Charles VII, who immediately ascended to the throne to replace his father.

However, considering the angel Gabriel's encounter with Mary, it may not be fair for the duke to claim ownership of coining that phrase just yet. When Gabriel informs Mary about her miraculous pregnancy by the Holy Spirit and the naming of her son Jesus, he also shares another extraordinary proclamation. He tells her that Jesus will ascend to the throne of his father David, and his reign will never cease, making him an eternal king.

The thing about earthly kings is that their reigns are destined to come to an end with their death. And while it's important to have a plan for succession, the unpredictability of the new king remains a factor. He has the potential to be a noble and resolute king, fiercely defending the country's morals and values, or he could become a feeble ruler, ultimately surrendering the nation to the enemy. In the end, every earthly king is flawed and far from perfect, just like any other human being.

God's desire is for us to have a king who reigns supreme above all other kings. A king who is humbly born and lives among his people, teaching them and giving them a glimpse of what life looks like inside his kingdom. A king who is willing to sacrifice his own life to free the people in his kingdom by paying the ransom demanded by his enemy. Then a resurrected king who triumphs over those enemies with a decisive blow, thereby ensuring eternal peace and delivering salvation to all those in his kingdom. Jesus, who is God in human form, is the perfect embodiment of that description. He is the King of all kings! Long live the King!

Week 4, Day 22
ANGELS FROM THE REALMS OF GLORY—A HISTORY

It was a quiet Christmas Eve in 1816, and James Montgomery reclined in his comfortable chair, his gaze fixed on the frosted windowpane. The gentle flicker of candlelight created a cozy and inviting atmosphere that illuminated his desk and cast a warm glow on his open Bible, revealing the words of Luke 2. At forty-five, Montgomery reflected on what some would consider his adventurous life. Orphaned at a young age, he eventually ran away and lived a nomadic life until ultimately finding success as a wealthy newspaper publisher, missionary supporter, humanitarian, and political activist who had also spent time in prison for publishing seditious material. But one thing that never changed in his life was a deep love for writing poetry. When he glanced back at his Bible, his attention was immediately drawn to verse thirteen and the captivating story of the angels proclaiming the birth of Jesus. In that moment, a surge of inspiration passed through him, sparking his desire to write.

Montgomery's parents, John and Mary, were devoted Moravian missionaries serving in the small town of Irvine Ayrshire, Scotland. It was there, on November 4, 1771, that their son, James, was born. In 1777 they returned to Grace Hill, an Irish Moravian community in County Antrim, the same community that had initially sent them on their missionary journey. However, their return was short lived as they soon felt a call to serve as missionaries to slaves on the island of Barbados, West Indies, in the Caribbean.

Believing the West Indies were unsuitable for raising a child, they made the decision to send their six-year-old son to the Moravian Seminary in Fulneck. Located near Leeds in West Yorkshire, the seminary would provide him with care and a classical education that would one day prepare him for the ministry. Over a span of nine years, he received a comprehensive education that included traditional English grammar school studies along with a wide range of subjects, such as ancient and modern sciences as well as German, French, Latin, and Greek.

The school, however, was not so diverse when it came to secular studies or even poetry, as both were banned at Fulneck. This posed a challenge for young James, who loved poetry and, by the age of ten, was already crafting his own verses. Additionally, his limited interaction with the outside world further isolated him. Despite the strict school rules, Montgomery still found ways to secretly read poetry, quickly realizing that his calling was to be a writer rather than a minister.

Undoubtedly his experience at Fulneck was an unhappy one, especially since he struggled academically and received negative progress reports from his teachers. Then, at the tender age of twelve, he received the devastating news of his parents' death due to yellow fever while serving on the mission field. Now an orphan and utterly depressed, his academic performance continued to decline, and teachers found him to be nothing more than a dreamer, lost in his own world. All he wanted to do was write poems and stories. Nothing else interested him. When he turned fourteen, the school deemed him unteachable and made the decision to withdraw him, ultimately apprenticing him to a baker.

Yet his apprenticeship didn't last long, prompting him to run away and find employment with a storekeeper in Wath-upon-Dearne, located thirty miles south. Unhappy with his job yet again, James ran away once more, this time to London. In the bustling city, he resorted to selling his poems on the streets, adopting a vagabond lifestyle during his teenage years. He couldn't find a suitable job, and despite his attempts to sell his poetry to publishers, his writing talents went unnoticed and he faced a string of rejections. He suffered periods of deep depression and would spend the next nine years in restless wanderings.

At twenty-three, he came across an advertisement for a clerk's position at the Sheffield Register newspaper. After applying for the job through a letter, he was offered employment and wasted no time in starting his writing journey. Both the paper and its owner, Joseph Gales, were somewhat controversial. Gales, who worked as a printer, bookseller, auctioneer, and editor of the paper, also had a penchant for stirring up political debate. He was frequently imprisoned for boldly advocating for Ireland's freedom from Great Britain. James quickly embraced the beliefs of his radical employer and became a passionate advocate for the rights of the people. Eventually Gales was driven out of town and fled to Philadelphia, leaving the newspaper without an editor.

In order to keep the paper alive, Montgomery took charge of it and secured funding from a wealthy townsman. At the young age of twenty-five, he began managing the paper, immersing himself in his work and fearlessly taking on various pressing issues of the day. After several years, Montgomery was able to completely pay off the purchase money for the journal. With that financial burden lifted, he eagerly entered the business as a general printer.

The citizens of Sheffield widely read the paper, and it thrived under Montgomery's guidance, making him a wealthy man. In order to appease the government's hostility, he changed the paper's name to the Sheffield Iris and adopted a more moderate political stance. However, what he believed to be in moderation was still deemed radical by the government, resulting in his imprisonment twice for advocating for the abolition of slavery. While serving his sentence, he dedicated himself to writing poems that would later be compiled and published under the title *Prison Amusements*.

He would continue editing the paper for thirty-one years, rising to become one of the most respected and honored men in Sheffield. But for Montgomery, his greatest reward came in the form of an opportunity to share his poems with the world, as he now had the means to publish them whenever he saw fit.

The most significant transformation in his life happened in 1814, when he fully embraced his faith in Jesus Christ. It was clear that he had been brought up in the faith and taught the principles of Christianity by the Moravians during his childhood. He always recognized the significance of faith but had never personally dedicated himself to it until that moment. His life underwent significant changes from that point forward as he started using his talents in poetry and writing to spread God's message. Montgomery's enthusiasm led him to write over four hundred hymns, placing him third among British hymn writers, after Isaac Watts and Charles Wesley. He also wrote twenty-two books, and his lectures on poetry made him widely recognized and respected throughout the country.

His personal dedication to Christian principles translated into public support for various causes, including foreign missions, the expansion of Sunday schools, and the dissemination of Bibles and tracts. In terms of his social views, he passionately advocated for the abolition of slavery and vehemently opposed the exploitation of children in dangerous jobs like chimney sweeping.

On that Christmas Eve in 1816, Montgomery found himself reflecting on his life, his newfound faith, and the world around him. When he read the angel's proclamation in Luke 2, something about it resonated with him in a way that it never had before. The words began to flow effortlessly from his pen as he raced against the clock to finish before the evening paper went to print. The day was coming to an end, but his hard work was about to bear fruit. Readers of the Sheffield Iris would eagerly open their newspaper to find a heartwarming Christmas poem called "The Nativity." This captivating and spiritually rich poem stirs up a profound sense of urgency and anticipation among the angels, shepherds, and wise men, compelling them to come and worship the newborn king.

While the poem had become a beloved favorite in Sheffield, it achieved greater fame when Montgomery republished it in *The Christian Psalmist* under the title "Good Tidings of Great Joy to All People" in 1825. However, it wasn't until 1867, thirteen years after Montgomery's death, that a blind organist finally incorporated the tune into the carol as we know it today.

An English composer, Henry Smart was a self-taught musician with a remarkable talent for organ music. He came from a musical family, with his father being a music publisher and his uncle being a prominent British conductor. He was the organist at several London churches and composed a diverse range of music, including an oratorio and an opera.

By the age of eighteen, Smart started to lose his eyesight, and by fifty-two he was completely blind. Despite this disability, he excelled as an organist thanks to his talent for improvisation and the help of his daughter, who wrote out the compositions for him. His most exceptional music was believed to be written in his later years.

Smart had heard Montgomery's poem sung by a choir but felt the melody that was used didn't capture the beauty and enthusiasm of the words. He thus felt inspired to write a fresh composition, which he titled "Regent Square," named after the Regent Square Presbyterian Church in London. Additionally, he is credited with renaming the carol "Angels from the Realms of Glory."

James Montgomery is a prime illustration of blending one's talents, abilities, influence, and finances with spiritual convictions. Given everything he had experienced, it would be understandable if he rejected the religious beliefs of his missionary parents. After all, his parents tragically died while serving God on the mission field, leaving him as an orphan. Then his zealous Moravian teachers lacked faith in his abilities to the extent of driving him out of school.

While he faced moments of doubt during his adolescence and adulthood, he eventually embraced Christ and devoted the rest of his life to writing poetry that reflected the divine insights he received. As a result, his timeless poems and hymns have found a home in the hearts of people worldwide, enduring for over 250 years. And like us, Montgomery faced hardships in life, but God transformed his past pain and experiences into a powerful call to worship that resonates with millions of believers every Christmas.

Angels from the Realms of Glory

Angels, from the realms of glory,
Wing your flight o'er all the earth;
Ye who sang creation's story,
Now proclaim Messiah's birth

Chorus:
Come and worship,
Come and worship
Worship Christ, the newborn King.

Shepherds, in the fields abiding,
Watching o'er your flocks by night,
God with man is now residing,
Yonder shines the infant light:

Sages, leave your contemplations,
Brighter visions beam afar;
Seek the great Desire of nations,
Ye have seen his natal star:

Saints before the altar bending,
Watching long in hope and fear,
Suddenly the Lord, descending,
In his temple shall appear.

Angels from the Realms of Glory – James Montgomery Version

Angels, from the realms of glory,
Wing your flight o'er all the earth;
Ye who sang creation's story,
Now proclaim Messiah's birth:

Chorus:
Come and worship,
Come and worship
Worship Christ, the newborn King.

Shepherds, in the fields abiding,
Watching o'er your flocks by night,
God with man is now residing,
Yonder shines the infant light:

Sages, leave your contemplations,
Brighter visions beam afar;
Seek the great Desire of nations,
Ye have seen his natal star:

Saints before the altar bending,
Watching long in hope and fear,
Suddenly the Lord, descending,
In his temple shall appear.

Sinners, wrung with true repentance,
Doomed for guilt to endless pains,
Justice now revokes the sentence,
Mercy calls you—break your chains:

Though an infant now we view him,
He shall fill his Father's throne,
Gather all the nations to him;
Every knee shall then bow down:

All creation, join in praising
God the Father, Spirit, Son,
Evermore your voices raising,
To th'eternal Three in One:

Week 4, Day 23
ANGELS FROM THE REALMS OF GLORY

Suddenly, a large army of angels appeared with the angel. They were praising God by saying, "Glory to God in the highest heaven, and on earth peace to those who have his good will!" Luke 2:13–14

The presence of angels brings a sense of wonder, awe, and even fun to our cherished Christmas traditions. For example, we take great joy in incorporating these heavenly beings in nativity scenes and outdoor decorations, baking scrumptious cookies shaped like angels, admiring cute children dressed as angels in Christmas plays, and, of course, imagining angels singing songs about the newborn Jesus. Sometimes I wonder if angels are surprised, or perhaps even appalled, by the extent to which they are incorporated into the festivities of Christmas.

We often overlook the fact that angels, despite being supernatural beings created by God, are not all-knowing. Think about it for a moment. They have been here since before the creation of the world, and although they were aware of a salvation plan, they didn't know how it would unfold. Interestingly, the angels' first shouts of joy weren't at the birth of Christ but when the world was first created. God tells Job in poetic imagery that the "morning stars sang together, and all the sons of God shouted for joy" when he laid the foundations of the earth.[1]

After experiencing the immense joy of creation, these angels were then filled with sorrow as they witnessed the once incredible paradise they had seen come into existence become tainted by sin, death, and decay. However, God had a plan to restore creation and rescue humanity, entrusting angels with an active role in the unfolding of salvation history. They became divine messengers, offering hope, direction, and comfort to those like Hagar, Lot, Abraham, Jacob, Moses, Gideon, David, Daniel, Elijah, and many others. They eagerly watched as history unfolded, anxiously waiting for the Promised One to appear.[2]

Then the long-awaited moment arrived! God summoned the angel Gabriel to deliver a message regarding the coming of the Messiah to both Zechariah, an elderly priest, and Mary, a young woman. The angels braced themselves for the moment they'd all been waiting for—the world's redemption. Then, as soon as Christ was born, another group of angels was sent to a Bethlehem hillside, where shepherds were watching over their sheep. The very same angels who sang over the world's creation were now given the honor of announcing with joy the birth of the Messiah, who had come to save the creation that was broken.

The angels would undoubtedly find it offensive to draw any attention away from the baby Jesus. Perhaps our focus should be on appreciating the angels' jubilant celebration of Christ's birth rather than getting too preoccupied with their presence. After all, they had waited the longest, and their patience was finally rewarded.

---

1. Job 38:4–7

2. 1 Peter 1:12

I can almost hear the celestial choir as angels from all realms of glory united with the large army of angels on that Bethlehem hillside, their voices soaring in a symphony of praises to God in a celebration unmatched since the dawn of creation!

Week 4, Day 24
SHEPHERDS, IN THE FIELD ABIDING

In him was life, and that life was the light of all mankind. John 1:4

P ablo Picasso, the renowned artist who shaped the art world during the first half of the twentieth century, once said, "Art is a lie that makes us realize the truth." In other words, art reflects the artist's interpretation of their own version of reality. It's a lie because it is not the actual reality but just a representation of it. But by presenting art as reality, it prompts us to notice and appreciate it, leading us to a deeper understanding of the actual truth.

This is the case with what became one of the most popular art forms in Western Christian culture starting in the fifteenth century, known as "The Adoration of the Shepherds." These nativity paintings essentially capture the moments that immediately follow the birth of Christ and generally feature shepherds gathered around the newborn baby along with Mary and Joseph. In addition, certain artists have opted to showcase different versions of this style, incorporating elements like animals, additional people, shepherds playing instruments, angels, and other distinctive features.

Many of the paintings also share a common trait in that they depict a nighttime nativity, with the infant Jesus as the only source of light who casts a radiant glow on the faces of those who have drawn near to adore him. The painting from 1622 by Gerard van Honthorst is my favorite because of its exquisite details and vibrant colors. In this painting, Mary tenderly leans over the baby Jesus, her hands carefully swaddling him, while Joseph calmly rests his hands on the head of a cow to her left. Three shepherds stand on Mary's right side, their expressions a mix of amazement, curiosity, and devotion.

The beauty and genius of these paintings lies in their ability to transcend reality while leading us to a deeper truth. Each artist aimed to combine the classic Christmas narrative of the shepherds from Luke 2 with the unconventional Christmas story of Jesus as the light force from John 1. The core message portrayed in these paintings is that the closer we draw to Jesus, the more his divine light will increasingly brighten and transform our lives.

Regrettably, darkness still plagues the world, a stark reality that the artists do not ignore. For example, in van Honthorst's painting, the absence of a background scene is striking, with only the darkness of the night being depicted. But the light of the Christ child is so powerful that not even the darkest night can extinguish it. The apostle John emphasized as much when he said, "The light shines in the darkness, and the darkness has not overcome it."[1]

The beauty of Christmas lies in its ability to remind us that no matter how dark life may become, the light of Christ will always prevail. As you draw closer to adore the Christ child this Christmas, may his brightness bring delight to your eyes and

---

1. John 1:5

warmth to your heart, and may you become a reflection of that light for all that journey through life with you.

Week 4, Day 25
SAGES, LEAVE YOUR CONTEMPLATIONS

Then He said to them, "Follow Me, and I will make you fishers of men." Matthew 4:19

Scripture reveals little about this group of foreign Gentiles whom we refer to as "wise men," which in Greek is translated "magi." This word originally referred to a group of Persian scholars that possessed an exceptional knowledge of astronomy and astrology and likely held positions as priests in Persian temples. Despite their idolatrous theology, these men embarked on a remarkably long journey, possibly spanning eight hundred miles round trip, in search of the King of the Jews. The financial burden of this trip would have been substantial, not to mention the inherent risk and dangers associated with traveling at this time. In a way, the wise men are the first to leave behind their familiar and comfortable lives, responding to Jesus' call to follow him no matter where he leads.

Throughout history, countless disciples of Jesus would follow the same pattern initiated by the wise men. The most vivid illustration of this occurred when Jesus called Peter, Andrew, James, and John to follow him. These were ordinary fishermen just trying to catch enough fish to support their families and fulfill their tax obligations. Scripture tells us that in the middle of a typical workday, Jesus called out to them while walking along the shoreline. Without hesitation, they abandoned everything to follow him.

No additional information was given about what we might consider a hasty decision. This prompts a multitude of questions to flood our minds, such as what motivated them to react in that manner? For that matter, how did both the wise men and the disciples manage to leave behind their families, work, and obligations so effortlessly and without hesitation…and with no specific destination in mind?

The next line of this Christmas carol might offer us some clarity: "Brighter visions beam afar." In other words, the carol suggests that for the wise men, they should abandon their worldly wisdom because the birth of Jesus exceeds anything they could have imagined. Their "contemplations" are simply reflections on the observations made in this world. Those contemplations might lead them to where he is, but Jesus is not of this world. He is the Desire of all nations, the Incarnate God, whose knowledge and understanding are beyond measure. They are being invited to seek true knowledge and wisdom that only God can provide!

Regarding the disciples, we need to carefully consider the specifics of Jesus' invitation, which included a promise to make them "fishers of men." Although they may not have fully comprehended the implications at the time, they certainly grasped the intricacies of fishing. To excel in fishing, one must possess patience, be willing to take risks, and put in considerable effort. But even more so, a skilled fishermen firmly believes that by continuously casting their nets into the depths, they will eventually be rewarded with a catch. It was this kind of faith that enabled them to understand that although they couldn't see where Jesus was leading them, they believed, like the wise men, that he offered a brighter vision of the future.

Jesus has the ability to connect with people wherever they are in life and communicate in a manner that they can understand. He recognizes their natural talents and abilities and uses them to bring honor to him. He did this with the wise men by drawing upon their vast knowledge of astronomy to guide them to him, where they worshipped and presented him with gifts. And he did this with the disciples by using the same fishing skills they had honed over many years to help lure others into following him. And he will do the same for us if we allow him to.

With the New Year approaching, where is Jesus leading you to follow him? Which specific knowledge, talents, skills, and abilities does he seek to tap into for the purpose of bringing him glory? Just like the wise men and disciples, you may not fully comprehend everything at first, but whatever daring step Jesus is urging you to take, it will be rewarding!

Week 4, Day 26
SAINTS, BEFORE THE ALTAR BENDING

"I will send my messenger, who will prepare the way before me. Then suddenly the Lord you are seeking will come to his temple; the messenger of the covenant, whom you desire, will come," says the Lord Almighty. Malachi 3:1

Maybe, just like me, you've been singing this carol your entire life, never pausing to question the identity of the saints Montgomery is alluding to in the fourth verse. One could easily assume that he's referring to the saints mentioned by the apostle John in Revelation during the Lord's second coming rather than his first.[1] However, I would like to present an alternative interpretation.

When you read all seven original verses in their proper context, it appears Montgomery is referencing a historical setting, as he did with the angels, shepherds, and sages. If that's the case, then who are the saints that are patiently waiting and hoping? In this context, it's reasonable to assume they are Simeon and

---

1. Revelation 6:9–11

Anna, the elderly man and woman who had been longing for God's Messiah to be born and redeem Israel.[2]

Simeon and Anna's unwavering faith in God's promise was evident as they eagerly awaited the arrival of the Messiah at the temple, just as Malachi had prophesied. In fact, they were there every day, dedicating themselves to prayer, fasting, and watching. And then, one glorious day, it happened, probably not exactly as they had imagined but in a way that left them in awe. The Lord did enter the temple but as a tiny baby being carried by humble parents.

As the Holy Spirit revealed the baby's true identity, Simeon and Anna were overcome by a mix of emotions, from surprise and joy to an overwhelming sense of thankfulness. In the temple where they had been watching for so long, they worshipped the child with hearts full of gratitude, offering praise to God. This supports my belief that when Montgomery wrote the fourth verse, he was referring to Simeon and Anna, as it seems to describe the rare moment when Christ was worshipped as a "newborn king" in the temple.

It's also possible that Montgomery intended to add depth to his poem by incorporating both the first and second Advent into the verse. It's not lost on me that while we look back at Simeon and Anna's faithfulness, they were looking forward to God's faithfulness. The knowledge of Malachi's prophecy shaped their lives, and they lived with the constant expectation that God would keep his word. Their focus remained fixed ahead, eagerly scanning the temple each day in hopes of catching a glimpse of the long-awaited Messiah, and their faithfulness was richly rewarded.

---

2. Luke 2:25, 38

I suppose history will judge us too. Just as we honor and celebrate the Lord's first Advent with Simeon and Anna, we should eagerly expect and faithfully await his second coming. Jesus will return once more, this time not as an infant born in humble circumstances but as a victorious King accompanied by the heavenly armies. His first coming went largely unnoticed, but his second coming will be impossible to miss as the call of God will resound, summoning all the saints to come and worship.

Week 4, Day 27
SINNERS, WRUNG WITH TRUE REPENTANCE

Then Simeon blessed them and said to Mary, his mother, "This child is the reason that many people in Israel will be condemned and many others will be saved. He will be a sign that will expose the thoughts of those who reject him. And a sword will pierce your heart." Luke 2:34–35

I'm guessing that until now, you haven't heard, read, or sung the fifth verse of this carol. In most hymnals, you'll usually only see the first four verses printed. That's probably because no one wants to sing carols about sinners being doomed for guilt and endless pain during the joyful Christmas season. It's somewhat of a downer. However, Montgomery's decision to include the fifth verse in his poem serves as a powerful reminder that the nativity has a deeper meaning beyond a sentimental portrayal of a sweet manger scene.

To truly grasp the significance of Christmas, one must experience it in the light of Easter morning. The reality is that the cross of Calvary casts a solemn shadow over the humble manger where the peaceful Christ child lies. One can almost imagine the elderly man, Simeon, his weathered hands cradling the newborn baby as he offers heartfelt praise to God for sending the light of salvation to the nations. Then, suddenly, the sheer joy coursing through his body comes to an abrupt halt as his mind is overwhelmed by visions of immense suffering. Although the exact level of insight Simeon received remains uncertain, he was acutely aware that this precious newborn baby he had just handed back to Mary would eventually bring her pain but would also save the world.

Christmas and Easter both convey the same core message: Jesus was born with a divine mission, and that divine mission was to sacrifice himself for our sins. From the moment Jesus was born until his death, he spent each moment walking the lonely road to Calvary to accomplish that mission, and nothing could deter him from it. The Incarnation was not just a supernatural event where angels, shepherds, and wise men celebrated God's coming to the world in the form of a baby. It was a divine plan orchestrated by God and carried out by Jesus to free mankind from the power of sin and death.

The invitation extended to us each Christmas is not just about visiting him at the manger but also to walk alongside him on the road to Calvary. This path leads to joy and ultimate happiness, but it demands sacrifice—a willingness to die to ourselves. Far too often, though, we sing with great passion about the wonder and joy of the Christmas season without truly surrendering ourselves to God. Yet our ability to experience true joy in both this life and the next relies on our willingness to do just that.

As your celebration of Advent comes to a close, remember that Christmas and Easter are part of the same story. That story captures the awe-inspiring wonder, pure joy, and mystery of the Incarnation. It also delves into the depths of horror, profound betrayal, and the darkest aspects of humanity during the crucifixion. But then it beautifully unfolds into a tale of astonishing amazement, boundless love, and overwhelming joy with the resurrection. It is the greatest story ever told!

Week 4, Day 28
COME AND WORSHIP, COME AND WORSHIP

Come, let us bow down in worship, let us kneel before the Lord our Maker. Psalm 95:6

It's obvious that while reading the gospel accounts of the Savior's birth on Christmas Eve in 1816, James Montgomery was drawn to what he viewed as a recurring theme of worship. As his imagination took flight, it painted a vivid picture of what it might have been like to embody each of these ancient characters, each with their own fascinating story to tell. But despite the differences in each of their stories, they all shared a common reaction when encountering the Christ child—that of worship.

In his study that evening, Montgomery stumbled upon a revelation that inspired him to share it with the world. He discovered that the worship of the Messiah's arrival on Earth began with a glorious display by angels, followed by a humble demonstration from shepherds, then an honorable expression by wise men, and finally the overwhelming awe of saints and the heartfelt repentance of sinners. Then, as if in one resounding voice, all of creation came together at the end to worship the Father, Son, and Holy Spirit. Essentially, James's simple poem crafted that evening suggests that encountering Christ the newborn King should inspire a sense of worship, regardless of who you are.

As you draw closer to Christmas, consider the objects of your devotion, and examine what you are truly worshipping. Do you prioritize the external factors of Christmas, like purchasing gifts, adorning your home, attending festive events, or managing a jam-packed schedule? If so, don't be too hard on yourself—it's easy to get caught up in the chaos and, yes, even the fun of the holiday season.

That's why I believe Montgomery's 250-year-old carol resonates so well with our modern times: It's a powerful rallying call to worship. Let's answer the call and ensure that we are truly worshipping Christ this Christmas. After all, he is the eternal King that all of creation acknowledges as being born into this world as our Savior and is deserving of our praise.

May Christ the newborn King be the focus of your worship this Christmas, filling your hearts with love, joy, and peace and enabling you to inspire others through your devotion.

God bless and Merry Christmas!

ABOUT ME

I never thought I would be an author...

In all honesty, I cringe when referred to as such. My hesitation has nothing to do with the worthiness of the profession...far from it! I've always considered authors to be wordsmiths hammering out brilliant novels or some profound work that comes from a deep need within their soul. This is not me.

My writing comes from a different need—the need to understand. For example, when reading the theological and philosophical works of C.S. Lewis, I found it difficult to understand. I considered that if I struggled with the books, then perhaps others did too. So, beginning with *The Screwtape Letters*, I created summary and discussion questions for each chapter. Before publishing it, I led the study at my church, refining it as I went along. I then continued the same process with my next studies on *The Great Divorce* and *The Problem of Pain*. My good friend, Dr. Steve Urban, did the same with his excellent study guide for *Mere Christianity*.

My wife challenged me to create a study guide for John Bunyan's *The Pilgrim's Progress*. Unfortunately, I just couldn't get past the archaic language of the original 16th century text. I even tried some of the more modern translations, but those, too, left me confused. Again, I considered that if I found it difficult to understand, then others probably did, too. So, I spent the next year and a half rewriting the book in modern English, along with an accompanying study guide. The book has since become an Amazon best seller!

I also created some Christmas study guides, first publishing one on the Charles Dickens classic, *A Christmas Carol*, and then one on my favorite movie, *It's a Wonderful Life*. I then created a devotional series around classic hymns, including *The Carols of Christmas* and *The Hymns of Easter*.

As a self-published author, I don't have the backing of a large publishing house for marketing and sales. So, if you enjoyed this book, please leave a review on Amazon. Most books get one review per thousand readers, so I would be infinitely appreciative if you could help me out. Your review will also help others know if this book is right for them.

I love waking up each morning knowing this is what God is allowing me to do. It's been truly a blessing for me and my family. But equally so is hearing from people all over the world who tell me how God has used one of these books to affect their life in some way.

I would love to hear from you too! You can contact me at BrownChairBooks.com. I respond to every email. Thanks again for taking a moment to get to know more about me and my books!

Free Resources
The Carols of Christmas

Discussion Guide

For book clubs, small groups, Sunday school classes, or family devotions, I've created discussion guides for each volume of The Carols of Christmas series. Each guide is designed to spark lively conversation and reflection, prompting deeper exploration of the themes in that week's reading.

Podcasts

Dive deeper into the rich histories behind some of the carols in each volume of The Carols of Christmas series. Surprisingly, I used AI to create these. I simply provided all the necessary details and was able to produce an informative podcast centered around the carols I wanted to showcase. Each podcast explores the carol's history and lyrics, with episodes lasting around 15 minutes. I think you will really enjoy these!

Additional Devotionals

Are you interested in more devotional content? I've written some extra weekly devotionals based on different carols, which I'll email to you. Check the "The Carols of Christmas" box during signup for extra content.

Download for Free Today!
www.BrownChairBooks.com/Free

The Carols of Christmas

Daily Advent Devotions on Classic Christmas Carols

Get All Three Volumes!

Volume 1

Carols include "O Holy Night", "I Heard the Bells on Christmas Day", "O Little Town of Bethlehem", and "Hark the Herald Angels Sing."

Volume 2

Carols include "Silent Night", "Joy to the World", "O Come All Ye Faithful", and "The First Noel".

Volume 3

Carols include "Come, Thou Long Expected Jesus", "It Came Upon the Midnight Clear", "What Child is This", and "Angels from the Realm of Glory."

www.BrownChairBooks.com

The Hymns of Easter

Daily Lent and Easter Devotions on Classic Hymns
By Alan Vermilye

The Hymns of Easter is a heart-warming devotional inspired by some of history's most cherished Easter hymns. Experience a fresh perspective on the hymns you've sung your whole life now set to personal reflections in this 40-day devotional journey.

The book contains 40 daily devotions perfect for celebrating Lent or Easter. Each week, you begin by reading the history of the hymn, followed by daily readings that reflect on a verse from the hymn along with Scripture and a devotion. The devotional is designed to start on Ash Wednesday and end the Saturday before Easter, but allows for flexibility within your schedule.

What others are saying:

"I highly recommend this book to all who want to make their time of Lent more meaningful. Loved it!!" Deborah

"An excellent historical account of Easter hymns. It's a great way to celebrate the Lent Season." Mike

"This book will stand right up there with his three Christmas devotionals as a way to reflect on the season and find the hope that these hymns offer!" Christina

www.BrownChairBooks.com

A Christmas Carol Study Guide

Book and Bible Study Based on A Christmas Carol

By Alan Vermilye

A Christmas Carol Book and Bible Study Guide includes the entire book of this Dickens classic as well as Bible study discussion questions for each chapter, Scripture references, and related commentary.

Detailed character sketches and an easy-to-read book summary provide deep insights into each character while examining the book's themes of greed, isolation, guilt, blame, compassion, generosity, transformation, forgiveness, and, finally, redemption. To help with those more difficult discussion questions, a complete answer guide is available for free online.

What others are saying:

"The study is perfect for this time of the year, turning our focus to the reason for the season—Jesus—and the gift of redemption we have through him." – Connie

"I used this for an adult Sunday School class. We all loved it!" – John

"This study is wonderful!" – Lori

"I found this a refreshing look at the Bible through the eyes of Ebenezer Scrooge's life." – Lynelle

www.BrownChairBooks.com

It's a Wonderful Life Study Guide

A Bible Study Based on the Christmas Classic It's a Wonderful Life

By Alan Vermilye

It's a Wonderful Life is one of the most popular and heart-warming films ever made. It's near-universal appeal and association with Christmas has provided a rich story of redemption that has inspired generations for decades.

It's a Wonderful Life Study Guide examines this beloved holiday classic and reminds us how easily we can become distracted from what is truly meaningful in life. This five-week Bible study experience comes complete with discussion questions for each session, Scripture references, detailed character sketches, movie summary, and related commentary. In addition, a complete answer guide and video segments for each session are available for free online.

What others are saying:

"Thank you, Alan, for the unforgettable experience. Your book has prompted me to see and learn much more than merely enjoying the film, It's a Wonderful Life." – Er Jwee

"The questions got us all thinking, and the answers provided were insightful and encouraging. I would definitely encourage Home Groups to study this!" – Jill

"It's a Wonderful Life Study Guide by Alan Vermilye is intelligent, innovative, interesting, involving, insightful, and inspirational." – Paul

www.BrownChairBooks.com

The Pilgrim's Progress Series

A Readable Modern-Day Version of the John Bunyan Classics

Get All Entire Series!

Part 1: Christian's Journey

Follow the epic adventure of Christian who leaves his home in the City of Destruction and begins a life-long quest to the Celestial City.

Part 2: Christiana's Journey

Follow the adventures of Christian's wife, Christiana, and her four boys, and a host of memorable characters who either help or hinder their progress on their journey to faith.

Part 3: The Life and Death of Mr. Badman

Depicts the stages of life—from cradle to grave—of a very wicked man in an evil age and the miserable consequences that undoubtedly follow such wretched living.

Study Guides Available for Each Book in the Series!

www.BrownChairBooks.com

The C.S. Lewis Study Series

The Most Trusted Study Guides to Learning the Works of C.S. Lewis

The Screwtape Letters Study Guide

A brilliant and satirical look at spiritual warfare and the dynamics of temptation.

Mere Christianity Study Guide

Become an expert on Lewis' most popular apologetics classic.

The Great Divorce Study Guide

This classic allegorical tale of heaven and hell will captivate you.

The Problem of Pain Study Guide

A philosophical approach to helping you find meaning and hope amid the pain.

www.BrownChairBooks.com

The Practice of the Presence of God

A 40-Day Devotion Based on Brother Lawrence's
The Practice of the Presence of God

By Alan Vermilye

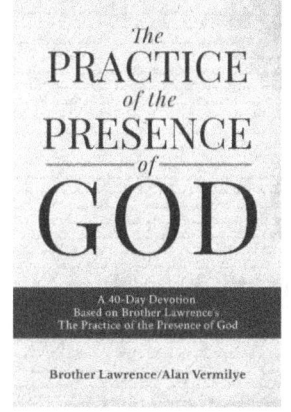

Since it was first published in 1691, The Practice of the Presence of God contains a collection of notes, letters, and interviews given by Brother Lawrence to his friends as a way of helping them turn ordinary daily life events into conversations with God.

Based on this timeless classic, The Practice of the Presence of God: A 40-Day Devotion guides readers on a 40-day journey through the wisdom of Brother Lawrence, related Scripture passages, and devotional thoughts that bring you into a more conversational relationship with God.

What others are saying:

"I love this devotional. It is short and to the point, and thus making it easy to stick to every day!" – Kathleen

"Enlightening new depths in prayer." – Kathy

"This devotional opens the door to Brother Lawrence that brings his letters and conversations to life every day!" – Steve

www.BrownChairBooks.com

www.ingramcontent.com/pod-product-compliance
Lightning Source LLC
Chambersburg PA
CBHW070151080526
44586CB00015B/1941